A Vacation in Baghdad and Beyond

Ardemis Donikian

Order this book online at www.trafford.com
or email orders@trafford.com

Most Trafford titles are also available at major online book retailers.

 www.trafford.com

North America & international
toll-free: 844 688 6899 (USA & Canada)
fax: 812 355 4082

Our mission is to efficiently provide the world's finest, most comprehensive book publishing service, enabling every author to experience success. To find out how to publish your book, your way, and have it available worldwide, visit us online at www.trafford.com

Because of the dynamic nature of the Internet, any web addresses or links contained in this book may have changed since publication and may no longer be valid. The views expressed in this work are solely those of the author and do not necessarily reflect the views of the publisher, and the publisher hereby disclaims any responsibility for them.

Any people depicted in stock imagery provided by Getty Images are models, and such images are being used for illustrative purposes only. Certain stock imagery © Getty Images.

ISBN: 978-1-4907-7671-2 (sc)
ISBN: 978-1-4907-7672-9 (e)

Library of Congress Control Number: 2022920022

Print information available on the last page.

Trafford rev. 02/06/2023

THIS BOOK IS DEDICATED TO THE CHILDREN OF IRAQ

IN THE PURSUIT OF HAPPINESS FOR THEM
Let Peace Prevail So We Can Grant Them a Virtuous Life
In my ideal world, no child should suffer.
And let nothing obscure their future.

"THE FATE OF A NATION DEPENDS ON THE EDUCATION OF ITS YOUTH"
Aristotle

Courtesy Aram Nabeel (Artist in Iraq)

Contents

WELCOME TO A VACATION IN BAGHDAD AND BEYOND 1

FROM "BAGHDAD BY THE TIGRIS" TO "BAGHDAD BY THE BAY" 2

BAGHDAD WAS CALLED 'MADINET AL SALAM' CITY OF PEACE HOTELS IN BAGHDAD 4

BAB EL WASTANI-CENTRAL ENTRY GATE TO BAGHDAD 6

A slice of my life – Reconciling the Past with the Present 8

My Parents Ohannes and Nevart Donikian 13

UNFORGOTTEN WORDS OF WISDOM – Past Teachings are essential today 15

HABITS OF IRAQIS 23

WOMEN AND MEN 28

ART OF MYSTIC COFFEE GROUND READING – GAHWA 31

 BREAKFAST IN THE CITY 39

HEARTY FLAVORS OF HOME - Let us bestow our lavish hospitality to you 42

THE NATIONAL MUSEUMS OF IRAQ - A GREAT CONTRIBUTION TO CIVILIZATION 49

GERTRUDE BELL & BAGHDADI WAX MUSEUM 52

KHAN MERJAN 55

NOSTALGIA ALONG ABU NAWASS STREET – FAMOUS FOR FISH 'MASGOUF' 60

AL FAW PALACE – 64

AL SHAHEED MONUMENT 67

THE UNKNOWN SOLDIER MONUMENT 68

MUSTANSARIYA UNIVERSITY 70

KERBALA & NAJAF 72

ZUMURRUD KHATOUN 75

SOUK EL SAFAFIR-COPPER MARKET 77

SPICE MARKETS BAHARAT 79

BLESSED MOTHER ARMENIAN CHURCH-MESKENTA 81

SWORDS OF QUADDASSIYAH – VICTORY HANDS 84

FLAT ROOFTOPS OF BAGHDAD - "Every Sunset brings a promise of a new dawn" Ralph Waldo
Emerson 85

BAGHDAD TOWER 89

MUTANABBI STREET المتنبي 92

MANNA – The Noblest of all Desserts 96

ABRAHAM'S WELL- EYN EL ASAD - A force of the desert 98

FLYING CARPETS 102

CTESIPHON – A residence to match the King's prestige 104

Welcome To Iraq" 107

Lion of Babylon 109

BABYLON – ONE OF THE SEVEN WONDERS OF THE WORLD - Civilization and knowledge still lie within its walls 110

Nabuchadnezzar Entry Gate... 112

PROCESSION STREET – BABYLON – The Street that launched civilization 114

Modern Palace on Euphrates-Offers a grand view of Babylon 116

BABYLON THEATER- MODERN FESTIVALS 119

BABEL TOWER 120

GREEK AMPHITHEATER- BABEL -SELEUCID ERA IN MESOPOTAMIA.. 122

NABUCHADNEZZAR AND THE HANGING GARDENS OF BABYLON- A highly developed society! One of the Seven Wonders of the World. 127

REVIVAL OF MARSH ARABS 131

CODE OF HAMMURABI-THE WISE RULER WHO INSTITUTED THE RULES OF LAWS - "Liberty is the right to do what the Law permits" Charles de Monteqlieu 137

EPIC OF GILGAMESH – QUEST FOR IMMORTALITY 139

SAMARRA – Once the capital of Iraq.. 142

UR – KINGDOM OF QUEEN PUABI 144

LAKE HABBANIYA 148

KIRKUK NORTHERN IRAQ 150

HATRA - Al Hadr- Once an Oasis City – In the barren landscape once rose an empire 152

BASRAH – CITY OF 'SINDBAD THE SAILOR' 154

ADAM'S TREE AT GARDEN OF EDEN – QURNA – South Iraq... 157

THE MAGIC TREE OF LIFE -"That which makes life worth living" 158

MOSUL 159

NORTHERN IRAQ – A magnetism for tourists.. 161

MONASTERIES IN NORTHERN IRAQ.. 163

WHY ARE ARMENIANS LIVING IN IRAQ AND NOT THEIR HOMELAND? 165

ALADDIN'S LAMP 170

MAKE A WISH 171

WELCOME TO A VACATION IN BAGHDAD AND BEYOND

مرحبا بكم في العراق

Let it be known that on examining the finds of ancient scrolls, it has been clearly deciphered and spelled out that whoever, at any time, dares to plunder or cause terror, will never rest in peace.

Just observe the endurance of the people of this land engulfed with the endless hovering forces of the desert which now leads them to the road of full recovery to anticipate better days.

FROM "BAGHDAD BY THE TIGRIS" TO "BAGHDAD BY THE BAY"

Why did Herb Cain, the famous San Francisco Chronicle columnist, nickname his beloved city of San Francisco, 'Baghdad by the Bay?'

My own artwork

He must have been fascinated and charmed by the mystery tales of the 1,001 Arabian Nights or perhaps Iraq's multi-cultural diversity.

Historical achievements and the mystery of the Babylonian Kings and its wise rulers must have influenced his intellect.

Most probably he associated the Golden Gate Bridge to the Golden Gate Palace built in Baghdad by Caliph Mansour which had majesty and realm. The Palace was colossal and of legendary beauty with its emerald, green dome reaching a height of 130 feet and visible from afar. To show his importance to his people, Mansour had a large statue built on top of the dome. It portrayed the ruler sitting on a horse, firmly grasping to a lit lamp which was visible from afar. It is said that it had an enchanting effect on those who remained in its light reminding them of his glory and his might.

In San Francisco 'Baghdad by The Bay', you can compare the Golden Gate Palace to the Golden Gate Bridge with its high span visible from afar, showing its presence, even on days when engulfed by a blanket of fog. Once upon a time many explorers sailed by the Golden Gate entryway along the Pacific coast, but the clouds obscured and restricted their visibility. They missed the entry into the Bay until its discovery in 1760 by the Portola Expedition. In comparison, Baghdad was also an impenetrable city surrounded by an immense circular moat.

The famous short story writer William Sydney Porter named his beloved city of New York 'Baghdad –on-the-Subway' which was later called 'Baghdad on the Hudson'. He had an imaginative mind and was also passionate about the Arabian Tales as one of his books was entitled 'Gift of the Magi'.

This is a learning experience and an adventurous journey as we embark to a place which has always been a modern metropolis. A place which seems so remote yet deserves recognition. You will be able to piece together stories about yesterday and today.

Our rivers do no longer wish to groan, the palm trees do no longer wish to sigh, the scars of war have to heal so that the silence on the horizon will allow the drifting sounds of lasting peace loom in the air as my people strive to live harmoniously.

BAGHDAD WAS CALLED 'MADINET AL SALAM' CITY OF PEACE
HOTELS IN BAGHDAD

ISHTAR SHERATON HOTEL - PALESTINE INTERNATIONAL HOTEL
AL RASHEED HOTEL - PALM BEACH HOTEL - AMBASSADOR HOTEL - KANDEEL HOTEL
MASBAH PALACE HOTEL - AL MANSOUR HOTEL - CORAL HOTEL -RIMAL HOTEL

I am ready to take you on an adventurous real-life journey and shed some light on my nation. You might be curious as to what lies beyond the news from the media, so please read on.

With a sense of nostalgia, I invite you to visit the major highlights of the country to gain insight and immerse ourselves in a world still unknown to many. We will travel back in time while memories of the past shall come alive as I recount experiences of my life in Iraq. I hope to enrich your knowledge about my nation. Please note that we were never ever deprived of anything in this prosperous country.

We have often heard of the ancient days of Babylon and more recently the upheaval of Iraq, formerly known as *'The Cradle of Civilization'*.

The world has known of the ancient wonders of this land for thousands of years. Most recently Iraq has been in the forefront of current events due to its existence in the shadow of unrest.

But do we really know about the culture and the life of an Iraqi? What kind of a city was Baghdad and what kind of incredible journeys are in store for an eager traveler once this land returns to its former glory.

This book will answer these questions enlightening the reader to the history and human heart of Iraq. I recount my experiences as a young person living in the great city of Baghdad during its golden hey-day. The factual anecdotes will provide a potential traveler with needed information and an overview of the country.

The short stories give insight to the reader through my memories and impressions and the soul of a nation that has until now often only been an anomaly to much of the world.

So come along on this magic carpet ride with me as your guide and you will learn and uncover a journey for the ages.

Baghdad City

BAB EL WASTANI-CENTRAL ENTRY GATE TO BAGHDAD

They say: "*all roads lead to Baghdad*"! We knew not of conflicts, nor wars, nor upheavals while we lived In Iraq, so it is important to reveal to the world the serene life we had. It is vital to point out that Iraqis have a lot of pride and they have faced hardship with fortitude in the last few years, as they strive for a higher purpose.

The only surviving entry gate of the four which surrounded the round city of Baghdad is called "Bab El Wastani " the "Central Gate". It still stands by Sheikh Omar Street and was built in 13th century, during the Abbasid era as one of the main access points to the walled city.

The important monumental gateway leading to the courtyard was an entrance to the city reserved for the elite, such as monarchs, princes, dignitaries, and higher officials. It was a majestic entry which was reached by crossing a draw bridge over a moat. It was built in baked bricks and surrounded with thick walls designed as a defense to deter invaders.

The central stairs lead to the main platform and to a domed large gateway flanked by massive walls on each side. It houses inner colonnaded vaulted arcades where most probably guarded sentinels stood. Another staircase leads to the projecting tower where slits in the earthen brick walls were used for the launching of cannon balls.

The entrances were always protected and could stand any threats or danger since the soldiers could hurl and fire from these armaments at long range. The tactics used were mainly to restrain and discourage the enemy.

Pyrotechnic fireworks were first launched into the air in order to scare horses with thundering sounds and light before launching the actual weapons.

One ancient cannon is still at the forefront of the building. It was mounted on wheels, easy to transport and manned by a couple of skilled infantry soldiers. There exists no more gunpowder to fuse and fire. It is now disabled and stands only for the purpose of everlasting history.

Here, without a key, you can unlock the gate which leads you to a voyage of discovery.

"War is what happens when language fails" Margaret Atwood.

A slice of my life – Reconciling the Past with the Present

سعيد يومكم

I am an Armenian born in the land between two rivers and I would like to tell you about my upbringing and my life in Baghdad.

The news media always mentions Baghdad, yet the world knows very little about the day-to-day life and its customs and traditions.

We were not born with sand in our eyes, we have not been lost in the midst of the wilderness, nor are we veiled from the world. We stand as a proud prosperous nation with a rich culture, two life giving rivers, lakes, and even mountains in addition to a great will to survive.

A little bit about me. As a child it was important to feel a sense of pride when I attained good grades. I was oriented towards education and followed a positive pattern for long range goals for a constructive future. To date being productive daily is one of my traits and I have to reach accomplishment by being ethical, gaining recognition and trying to make the world a better place for all.

My family would always tell me that the day I came to life, I brought good luck to the household. Maybe I can grant you some luck also while you read this book.

I was born with a passion for reading, music and dancing and I just adored my pets. I always tried to find the time to pick up a book and drift away to another realm. We used to go to my favorite spot 'Coronet Bookstore' at Tahrir Square. I was always delighted to enter the establishment, absorbed in the comforting aroma that surrounded me. Here, the scent of new and old books diverted my mind and gave me inspiration. I spent a lot of time perusing the old and the new volumes which would help me in every aspect of my day-to-day life. I also enjoyed magazines and comic books to broaden my horizons and be up to date with the entertainment world.

All this would stimulate my mind, improve my vocabulary, and develop my writing skills. I felt I became more knowledgeable and improved my quality of life.

At this bookstore, they also sold 45 rpm vinyl records which were imported from Europe and the USA, and my family bought as many as I could carry. At home, in a relaxing atmosphere I took great pleasure in picking up one of the books and listening to the new songs, always in the company of my lovely dog 'Ponti', my best loyal affectionate friend. I will always love and protect animals.

I stress the point that "*the greatness of a nation and its moral progress can be judged by the way its animals are treated.*"- Mahatma Gandhi

Even nowadays in times of stress I reach out to music as it has a healing effect on my psyche, and immediately changes my outlook and alters my moods. It has been my therapy to help me heal faster after surgical procedures as it eased the pain and gave my immune system a boost. Nowadays the effect of music surrounding me uplifts me as I continue to benefit, excel, and enjoy.

I feel motivated to sway with dance steps to the rhythm of any music. It has helped me become flexible. It rejuvenates my mental skills as I try to remember the complex dance steps. This activity always puts me in a good mood and all tension disappears.

My life and upbringing in this city will remain vivid forever in my thoughts as I travel through time to a place where we led a privileged life without any limitations.

My Mother and I

Baghdad is classified as the third largest city in the Middle East, a place where my early childhood and teenage years blossomed. We lived a comfortable life, for this was the land where Armenians had a chance to accomplish their purpose of existence.

The kingdom of Iraq was established in 1921. The League of Nations gave Great Britain the mandate to rule the country and thus established the monarchy of the Hashemite Kingdom, which crowned King Faisal I in August 1921 as the monarch. The country was then given independence in 1931. The only British legacy left is the double-decker public transport red buses which are still rolling in the streets of the capital. The monarchy lasted until 1958 when a revolution ended this phase.

Baghdad was built as a round city by Caliph El Mansour on the western part of the Tigris, and quickly expanded to the east side. Rusaffa and Karkh are linked now by many bridges. It was a wealthy metropolis and the focal site for academic growth and learning, where renowned individuals came to develop their college training.

My family and I first lived on the eastern side, Bab El Sharji, (east gate) in a spacious house consisting of two floors, with four bedrooms, two living rooms, dining room and a vast garden in the back. Our house faced "Umma Gardens" which was a large public park with manicured green lawns and exotic flowers, a large pond with fountains and colorful spotlights which glimmered at night. Once the sun set, the park was filled with people and became our nightly entertainment. After a few years, we moved to Mansour City.

We had Arab Sunni, Arab Shia, Kurds, Assyrians, Chaldeans and Turks living on our street, and were not only neighbors but also friends. There was always peace amongst us, and we all reached out for each other and gathered for dinners and parties. Never did I see disaccord or animosity, so what has happened in the recent years really bewilders and disheartens me.

Our House in Mansour City   Elegance at Wedding
                                     Service in Baghdad

I studied at College Du Centre -'Soeurs De La Representation', a school located in the midst of winding old alleys off Rashid Street. It was a large modern complex run by Catholic nuns where I learned French and improved in English (since I already spoke the language I had learned whilst living in Cyprus). It was an international school, a strict one, where good grades were a necessity and perseverance prevailed.

I studied hard with an aim to succeed. I strived for perfection and tried to make good use of time. Learning several languages at one time was a hard chore but I looked forward to attaining good results so that my family would be proud of me. Later I left for Lebanon, Beirut and attended Middle East College Sabtieh Bourchrieh, situated on Mount Lebanon with the most beautiful panorama of the city of Beirut. I continued my education at Pitmans College in London, worked as an office assistant at British Oxygen Company, and eventually went to Milan, Italy and worked for Johnson Wax Company, then Saccab Inc. Trezzano Sul Naviglio.

My children Manuel and Sevan were born there too. After thirteen years we decided to move the United States. *"Life is a journey not to be forgotten."*

My Parents Ohannes and Nevart Donikian

My father Ohannes was employed at the Iraqi Petroleum Company in the Industrial Relations Department. He was responsible for the legal translations, cost of living index and supervisions of the implementation of Iraqi Social Security Legislation relating to Baghdad/Mosul/ Basra Petroleum Companies.

Later he became a diplomat and worked for the Ministry of Foreign Trade in Baghdad. He traveled to many countries and met many Heads of States. On his departure from the Ministry, he was granted the impressive 'Award of Recognition'.

He remained very proud of his nation, and I remember him saying to us *"We are fortunate to be living in Iraq, the whole world is at war, yet we live in peace here, it is also a promising land of opportunity."*

My mother Nevart had high standards and became a well-known hairstylist and make-up professional. Her clientele included foreign ambassadors' wives and dignitaries; she was very successful and managed two hair-salons: 'Salon Du Barry' and 'Alf Leyla Wa Leyla'. Every year she traveled to Europe to advance in her skills with an extensive training to broaden her knowledge and brought new upgraded equipment for her businesses.

Both of my children are talented. My son Manuel is an assistant librarian and composes his own music and lyrics, well known for his acting career in theaters in the Bay Area, also he is endowed with a great sense of humor.

My daughter Sevan is an experienced hairstylist and follows her singing career with her own band and possesses clairvoyant skills.

"Always promote harmony in the family, and you can't go wrong."

UNFORGOTTEN WORDS OF WISDOM
– Past Teachings are essential today

My Godfather Ohannes, aunt Zevart, grandmother Azniv, grandfather Donik

The Human Clock. Grandmother Azniv

I really feel that the only person, who loved me unconditionally when I was young, was my grandmother (Nene) Azniv. She was a nurturing person with a kind soul and a heart of gold. I was really attached to her and her wisdom. I truly enjoyed her company and each time I visited her, I learned something new.

She used to say *"waste no time, nor remain idle, because as we sit in comfort, my mind remains alert as I have learned to determine and predict the time by just looking at the length of the shadow on the walls and floor in the courtyard"*. She was the 'human clock' and I found it fascinating, so I repeatedly, throughout the day, asked her what time it was. She would lean against the window and look outside and, with a smile on her face, define the exact time in hours and minutes, which always amazed me!

Her specialty was cooking rice pilaf. She would pour two cups into a flat tray and then spread some and pick up the little stones from the rice. She would then say: *"These are the impurities that you need to get rid of, and in your life, when you feel you have undesired challenges, discard them immediately."*

On certain nights in spring, while she prepared home-made delicious 'halva' (a sweet dessert), with melancholy in her eyes, she would say: *"This aroma reminds me of the shady paths of our fruit trees in my hometown in Erzurum and the sweet scent in the air, all confiscated by the Ottoman Turks. Everyone and everything they destroyed."*

While I truly enjoyed each bite of the halva she had prepared, I would feel her wistfulness whilst I hugged her. I was her persuasive power who made certain she ended up with a smile on her face.

My dedication to her:" *When she walks, she casts a shadow of purpose, which radiates comfort and gentleness. May joy follow her soul as her own shadow*."

The Sparrow

The tales from my grandfather Donik never ended. As we would sit on the steps of the shaded portico in the courtyard, he would tell us his favorite story of the sparrow, whilst we savored the most delicious mulberries we had picked from his tree. He always spoke about the vast orchards belonging to his family in Diyarbakir-Turkey, also seized by the Ottoman Turks.

The sparrows chirped happily on the branches of the huge mulberry tree and seemed to have gathered for a rendez-vous. *"See how elegantly they are perched on the tree"*, he said, *"they are united and keep complete balance, they are classified as messenger birds, protecting this beautiful fruit tree which sustains the best fruit on its branches"*.

"Their presence is beneficial as they eat the insects in the air, and watch as we get closer, how concerned they are about each other's safety, they work together to protect their nests. They do not remain indolent, they continuously keep themselves busy picking up dry leaves, twigs and grass and paper to fortify their nests which they build in the corners of the outer walls. It is known that their presence is a good omen as

they symbolize good luck".

He continued saying: *"So never ever tell a lie or commit a crime, because these messenger birds will fly to report everything, and through them we can find out the truth".* I would nod my head and humbly accept his statements. When I asked him how he knew the answers to all my questions, he would say, *"Well, the sparrows just told me, secrets always come to light through them."*

Thus, I learned how to have a connection with the sparrows. We had several citrus trees which the birds were particularly attracted to. At sunset, a flock would gather and sing loud in chorus, they sounded lively and rhythmic as they seemed to announce their presence to defend their territory. It was pleasant to hear the melodies and I would replicate their sounds while feeding them. They were so fascinating, alert and showed no fear as they chirped continuously and brought life to our backyard until it got dark. When we picked the fruit from these trees, it always tasted delicious, and we made a special nutritious, tangy sweet 'welcome' drink from the pulp which we consumed all year round. Thus, I explained to our guests that this was a special beverage rendered tasty simply by the presence of sweet-sounding sparrows.

When we sat in the courtyard, there was grass growing all around his mulberry tree. Grandfather would reach out to pick a long flat wide blade, tear a small open space, place it in between his two thumbs, and then blow through the tiny opening, thus creating a whistling sound. We tried to imitate him, but we never managed to reproduce the same pitch. He would remain amused and continue to encourage us to keep on trying until we attained the same sounds. *"Practice until you become perfect and learn to persist until you reach your purpose."*

In the evenings he always found the time to enjoy a glass of 'Arak'. He poured the clear anise flavored liquor in a glass. He would say to me *"watch the magic while I pour water over it!"* Sure enough the transparency turned into a cloudy white shade. I always took the first sip and enjoyed the tingling fresh taste and sweet aroma, while he then delightfully continued to sip the beverage. "Only Arak," he said, *"eases the tensions of the day, and puts you in a good mood."* Until today, it remains my favorite potion. When we had a toothache, we would rub our gums with the liquid as it would numb the pain and, on certain occasions, used it as a flavorful antiseptic.

Holding On to Memories

In the hot summer months, the sky was always clear and the heat intense. The hope of catching the faintest breeze outside was unconceivable, so everyone stayed in their homes with the air- conditioners, air coolers and fans on full blast. Towards the late afternoon, my maternal grandfather Ohannes, also known as Yunnis Agha (he had a noble title), would take us out for chilled pomegranate juice and ice cream. As I grumbled about the unbearable heat, he would say: "*Stop complaining child. While we cross the bridge, close your eyes tight, release your mind of negative thoughts. Relax, take a deep breath and imagine the refreshing air arise from the fresh flowing river, as soon as we are on the other side, you will feel cooler.*" At that moment, I wish I could have pushed the river to create a forceful current to render a swifter tide to curb the heat, because I could also feel the heels of my shoe ensnare into the melted asphalt. I had no choice but to create a mental image which gave me the ability to sense the circumstances differently.

I learned thereby the power of autosuggestion. In any situation I could concentrate on optimistic thoughts, direct them to the subconscious mind, create a mental picture repeat and imagine it, set these thoughts in motion with persistence and make things happen. The power of imagination can attract whatever you desire because you can master your thoughts, with a positive forward-looking attitude.

I then also said to grandfather "*I can envision the solution for this land of eternal sunshine! When I grow up, I will delve into a plan that will create a comfortable setting for the city. I will plant, as far as the eye can see, different layers of thousands of fast-growing palm trees that can endure this heat. These will add an exotic beauty to the landscape and its flowing fronds will block the sun. They will act like a towering umbrella canopy which will create an everlasting cooling effect with no direct sunshine, whilst the light will filter and gently flow graciously through its leaves.*"

Thinking from the point of view of a teenager I used to intrigue him. Then he would ask me "*so how would you irrigate the soil?*" I had to always think twice then I would answer: "*Oh, there is a yearly overflow of flood rainwater so we can find a way to collect and harvest it. An irrigation system with sprinklers and canals to direct the flow of the water from the river into reservoirs, to also collect and store for future use.*"

In fact, vast extensive stretches of bare land can be transformed into an oasis. These trees would also help to block and reduce the dust storms from fully permeating into the city, which would be a 'welcome relief'. He was pleased with my answer and patted me on my head. *"Imagination can unlock the power of possibility." Eric Liu.*

He was always eager to educate me about his past, so he said *"Once upon a time people used to cross this river on floating pontoon bridges. These were an array of boats and barges tied and connected together to support a deck on which people walked to cross the river, but it could not support too much of a load and was dangerous."*

Also people travelled in circular boats called 'Kufas'. They would go to the riverside front to watch the artisans build them. They resembled large round baskets made of the ribs of palm leaves and reeds intertwined with a framework of ropes. The bottom was flat made of stretched animal hide and covered with bitumen for water resistance. Now at the British Museum you will see sculptured panels dating back thousands of years, belonging to the Assyrian Empire which show the same type of vessels used then.

"They rowed the round boat with a paddle, and you would have to be an expert to maneuver it, otherwise the vessel would spin. The people would carry and trade their merchandise on the shores as this was their only means of transportation. Nowadays, listen to the hum of the river which has also changed."

He was a humorous man, but quick to anger, so in his presence we would not attempt anything to upset him. We had a high regard for grandfather as he groomed himself daily. He always wore neatly ironed suits and had various hats which matched and made sure he polished his shoes. I believe that was his attempt to demonstrate that anyone can add a 'spark' to their 'persona'.

Metz baba was a man of distinguished qualities who recounted stories and adventures of his wealthy family profession involved in the transportation industry. The family owned several horse-drawn carriages for the extensive post-office delivery of mail and packages along the Silk Road. They were renowned for excellent service as they contributed generously to the Armenian and Turkish communities. They were highly esteemed in the city of Kilis in Turkey and employed several Turks. One day a few them who were loyal and dedicated coachman drivers approached his family and advised them secretly to leave the town immediately as there was going to be a new ruling by the government to persecute all the Armenians.

The Manougian Family thus collected all their belongings and business gear and left for Aleppo Syria. They owned a mail delivery service consisting of several horse-drawn carriages which would journey for several days from Kilis to Aleppo in Syria, then head to Baghdad, Iraq. They set up a reliable postal delivery and courier business with a postmaster and several coachmen and guards to distribute correspondence, mail and packages to several cities. The established trade route was familiar to them and so they were able to prosper since they were famed for their loyalty, upkeep, and servicing of their industry.

During their voyages, the family business owners noticed the quality of the road conditions had to be improved for a faster and more efficient delivery. As time went by, they were not impressed with the thoroughfares which were uncomfortable and steep because they had to stop several times to rest their horses and, at times, the heat was unbearable, and the coachmen felt exhausted and weary. This is when my grandfather and his family thought of changing their type of business and focusing more on the construction of new roads. They knew that the governments were developing and expanding a new railway system, adding small commercial river traffic which would eventually restrict their mail delivery industry.

So once again they moved to Kirkuk in Iraq where they were offered greater opportunities in the building of a network of roads leading all the way to Northern Iraq-Kurdistan.

After unfolding his story, he remained pensive and silent with an air of contentment because they had provided a prosperous life for the family. My mother would point out that she remembered when they brought home several large 45-pound tins full of currency and gold coins which then led them to affluence.

I remember my grandfather as a man who had a passion for smoking a water pipe. In our house, I would sneak behind the door and watch him as he would dampen the tobacco which he would carefully pull out of his colorful tins. He would then fill the base glass jar with water, adjust and connect the clean hose and mouthpiece and place the glowing hot charcoal over the to be immersed in another happy world, content to have some moments of leisure. As soon as he would notice me, he would smile and ask me to sit down and watch the bubbles as the water gurgled. He inhaled and then exhaled letting the smoke dissipate with a vaporous sigh, while the sweet smell of apple flavored tobacco floated in the air. I was impressed so I asked him if I could create the bubbles too. He would grin and say, as he handed me the mouthpiece, "*Here you go, try it yourself*". Well, I did, and surprisingly, nearly choked. So, from then on, I decided it was a pleasure just to watch him enjoy his simple distraction from life, whilst he repeated: "*Don't ever smoke your life away.*" As a man who believed in discipline and righteousness, he had the dreadful experience of facing deceit by his son in law Ibrahim Darwish who cheated and stole most of his earnings. "*Do NOT trust all people easily, you will regret it*", he would say sternly.

The Power of The Mind

Metz Mamma Esther, my maternal grandmother was a gifted spiritualist; she was well known as the woman with the sixth sense. She was Intuitive with supernatural skills in foretelling the future. She simply answered questions by consulting the Holy Scriptures in her Bible. She would randomly pick a page after a short prayer in Armenian, pinpoint a paragraph of her choice and give the answer. She could sense the aura of the person, pick up their energy, and direct her mind to her higher senses. She would listen to her inner voice which always gave her a great perception of people's future. The waves of telepathy and extra sensory perception allowed her to solve many people's problems. She became the most trusted mentor and adviser. She then passed on her natural gift to me I now cherish my psychic abilities and have put my power at work to the benefit of mankind. Daily results from my clients are all inscribed as testimonials in my diaries.

She would add these words of comfort: "*Be grateful in life, and cause no animosity, exercise tolerance and endurance during challenging moments, always look at the future with a positive approach.*"

When we would wake up in the morning, she would say with persistence every day: *"Do not roam around in your night gown or robe, embellish yourself, and look as best you can from the minute you are awake, <u>because a very important person may knock at your door anytime</u>."* These words exerted a very strong influence over me as I still apply them in my daily life. As she hurried up early morning to do her daily chores, she stressed also, *"in life, you have to make sure that you have no time to submit to boredom."*

"You can develop patience" she would say, as she gently placed a pot full of cold water on the stove. *"Now, just sit still, don't move until the water boils, stay tranquil and cultivate good thoughts"*. I had to obey. Time did not seem to pass, I wanted to reposition myself, but I was under her watchful eyes. She smiled and said with a low voice, *"You cannot get immediately what you want in life, but with time and the wisdom of patience, you can attain your goal"*. Since we could not accelerate this process, she taught us how to unwind, remain calm and learn to be persevering in life. And I believe that in today's fast paced world, we are constantly in a hurry to seek instant gratification and expect immediate results while we miss out on the simple pleasures of life. I also learned to practice self-discipline and to filter my words wisely before I uttered them.

Certain days grandmother would convey inspirational and spiritual messages, so I would try to decipher their meaning. One day she uttered silently: *"I dreamt of the dark angel of war encircling the map of Iraq, causing conflict and upcoming sufferance for its people, in years to come!"* We did not always heed to her words but as years went by, her prophecies all came true.

In the early stages of their arrival in Iraq, when her family had fled from Turkey, our family together with other Armenians and wealthy Arab neighbors founded a hospitality house, called 'Hokidoun' (meaning 'The Soul House'). They helped the homeless, hungry and forsaken Armenians who had escaped the genocide. They embarked on a task to venture to assist them in every way by placing them in these lodgings.

"I have often regretted the words I have spoken, but I have never regretted my silence" St. Arsenius the Great.

HABITS OF IRAQIS

Worry Beads - Tassbihs are used for leisure, to alleviate stress. Every household has one as it is an engaging habit for men in Iraq. They congregate at the coffee shops or at home as they hold the strand of beads in their hands, while they clip and click each bead in a repetitive manner.

The recurring action becomes habitual and helps a person unwind. It creates a channel of meditation by the soft clicking repetitive rhythmic sound. There is a misconception to the name 'worry beads', and the explanation lies in the fact that it literally soothes and relaxes the nerves. In other words: *"the beads are meant to take your worries away."*

Khamssa –Hand of Fatima. Since Iraqis are superstitious, it is a custom to hang this beautiful ornament on the wall, at the entrance of the home. It is believed that this amulet keeps the evil away and protects and guards the household. It attracts the good forces and erases negative energy. It even has the force to deter ill intentions of people and ward off malicious thoughts. It is also a trend nowadays to wear Khamssa jewelry around your neck so as to bear good fortune and wellness.

The five fingers represent the five pillars of Islam which are faith, prayer, to donate to the poor, to fast at Ramaddan and to go on a pilgrimage to Mecca

Blue Eye Beads - Protection against misfortune When a child is born, jewelry with beads is immediately attached to the clothing. It is a good luck talisman which defies evil forces, a symbol of protection and safety; it also wards off negative energy, danger and bad luck and brings wellbeing from the day the child is born.

This good luck charm in the form of jewelry is worn by nearly everybody as we believe in its power to safeguard us daily. Large blue-eyed ornaments also decorate our houses to bring safety.

Courtesy to the Host - As you know hospitality is literally unparalleled in Iraq, so when you visit a family, they will always serve either coffee or tea in a tray. When you are being served, you should pick the middle cup, so as to bestow bliss to the family.

<u>Travel</u> - If anyone had to travel by car, a bucketful of water is poured over the car whilst saying a short prayer for safety sake.

<u>Humor</u> - Do as I do, take life like a grain of salt. Then add laughter to it. It has a healing effect on your mind and your body. It invigorates the whole system whilst it relieves tension.

Ask any Iraqi if he knows any jokes, and he will definitely say: "*Which one would you like to hear?*" Daily amusing stories, "Noukte", were the norm of the day. How could we go through life without laughter? In the daily turmoil and stress of life, humor is a necessity. It erases our aches and pains and our daily outlook of our existence. Any Iraqi would say that the crisis of today is the joke of tomorrow. So reap the benefits and follow the quote of Mark Twain which says: "*against the assault of laughter nothing can stand.*"

I think that life, as a whole, is a "*laughing matter*", everything is solvable especially if you approach it with optimism. Even physical pain is known to heal with laughter. Try it and you will see that it scatters the tension and stress and brings relief. "*Nothing erases unpleasant thoughts more effectively than concentration on pleasant ones.*" Hans Selye

<u>Fabric Stores</u> - It was really fun to go to the souk with different shops, where vast arrays of fabrics were neatly displayed on the shelves. The vendor picked the rolls of material, and when you decided what to buy, he would take the scissors and say "Mabrouk" meaning "May you wear this with joy". Here was a stranger who was extending his good wishes upon you.

<u>Cordiality</u> - It is considered very disrespectful to cross your legs and display the sole of your shoes. The shoes are considered unclean. And you will never see a middle easterner place their feet with shoes on any table. Wherever you pray and when you enter a mosque, shoes must be removed.

<u>Manners at the table</u> - In my home, during meals, we all waited for everyone to sit at the table. We said a prayer of gratitude and then we started our meal. It was essential to have manners at the table. It was important to be polite and not interrupt but carry on a conversation which was going on by the elders. Rules of etiquette were a must.

<u>Cinemas</u> - Iraqis are movie lovers. There were many cinemas and I had passion for learning about the lives of famous actors and actresses from Hollywood. The films were mostly new releases in their original language with subtitles and it was a great way to discover another world beyond ours.

I never went alone or with my friends, I was always accompanied by one of the older members of the family. Just before we left the house we called and reserved a 'lodge'. It was a private booth on the second floor of the theater with four or six chairs to accommodate families. It was not a custom for females to sit amongst the public. I remember the new theaters were spacious, well-lit, and air-conditioned with ultra-modern comfortable seats and well-designed settings. Cinema Khayyam was considered as the best in the mid-east.

In the summertime open-air cinemas were considered a great outdoor event. It was sheer pleasure to watch the films under the moon and the stars.

The large screens and the sound system, even at that time, were added features to the movie going experience. *"Learn to delight and appreciate the simple pleasures of life."*

<u>The National Theater</u> – Tahrir Square, Karrrada - Famous for comedies, dramas and musicals, this theater offers a great deal of delight to the Iraqi people. It was closed for several years and is now open again with musical performances and entertainment for the public. The National Symphony Orchestra takes part together with national and international bands to bring a smile once again to the Iraqis. The ongoing famous play **"To Enjoy The Sweetness You Must Taste The Bitterness"** has been playing for several months. Theater is popular entertainment in this nation.

<u>Visiting</u> - You never go empty handed as a visitor, it is lack of respect. The item which is very much appreciated is a box of Manna. Another sweet delight is 'Lokum', a delicious chewy confection made with starch and sugar flavored with rose water, pistachios and walnuts and dusted with powdered sugar.

<u>Iraqis believe in Dreams</u> - In our family we paid attention to our dreams as a form of guidance. We do believe that they carry a message and can be prophetic. Dreams are symbolic of what lies ahead and serve a purpose and bear a meaning in our lives.

The unconscious mind stores plenty of dormant information which comes to life during the sleeping cycle. As you journey into a different realm, you relax and release tension. This is the reason why a good night's sleep is essential.

The brain still remains active as it creates vivid visual images which are influenced by the latest occurrences in your life. They reflect and carry insightful meaningful messages which have to be identified and interpreted as they may reveal a message or a warning. Sometimes it is difficult to decipher the meanings, so I am giving a few explanations which might help you understand your dreams.

<u>Stairs</u>: means reaching higher ranks, you will prove to yourself and others that you will elevate your status.

<u>Mother</u>: a sign of protection and safety. A sense of belonging lies in your desires, reaching out for maternal love, if any members of your family contact you, reach out to them.

<u>Dying</u>: a good omen, it represents an extension to your life. With willpower improve your health and your life because you have long years ahead.

<u>Slipping or Falling</u>: is a negative sign, unsuccessful status, failing in your life or your career, you are heading towards the wrong direction. It is unsafe to proceed unless you change. Better yourself.

<u>Confused dreams</u>: means to use wisdom in your speech. Learn to think before you speak. It is unwise to express your opinion sometimes. Refrain from criticism and gossip. Use sound and positive judgment, otherwise you will face problems. "*Give every man thy ear, but few thy voice*" Shakespeare.

<u>Plane</u>: indicates a journey or a transition from one location to another. Go on a vacation.

Weeping/Sadness: Time to regain self-confidence and will power to stand up to your rights. This indicates that being assertive and solving situations timely is essential. Think logically.

Child: Sign of innocence. Probably the birth of a child in family. Creation of a new life, venture or business. You seek nourishment and love and attention, which is lacking in your life, so give back the same.

Car or Train Accident: Avoid traveling. Cancel your trip. If you have to commute, be alert on the roads whilst driving. It would be wise to change travel itinerary for the time being. It is unwise to make a move at the present time.

Dove, birds flying: Signify a flight away from your daily life. There should be the desire to change your life and to launch yourself to higher dimensions.

Rainbows: mean your dull life will be enlightened, after the chaos, there is hope.

WOMEN AND MEN

Discretion and dignity are important for women in Iraq. This is a country where women are now more emancipated but still have to hold high values and morals.

It was a difficult experience for me to grow up in a very protective strict family where I was not granted any freedom. It was difficult because I was a student in the French School, off Rashid Street, run by Catholic nuns 'College du Centre – Soeurs De La Representation', and here I would listen to the tales of my school friends and felt they had to consider themselves very lucky to enjoy their freedom.

In Iraq a woman must dress modestly but there was no strictness to dress code. We were not forced to wear the "abaya", a black cloak that covered you from head to toe, nor did we wear a veil. We just dressed decently and acted inconspicuous especially in a male environment. Going downtown it was imperative to wear dresses with sleeves, and skirts below the knees. We would be respected and not bothered by the stares of the local men.

Women were allowed to drive and had the most up to date cars. Dating was not allowed and the partner in their life was usually chosen by family members. This factor is changing but flirting in public then with the male gender was considered offensive. Women were not allowed to go out with a man until you were officially engaged to him.

Now women live a different life, have adopted important roles in society and are engaged in many professions. More opportunities are unfolding. Importance is granted to their capabilities and they are more advantaged than before. Lately women have the right to vote and have the right to express their political views as everyday restrictions are slowly disappearing.

I grew up in a disciplined home and I try to teach my own children the importance of living a full life with integrity and fulfilling essential duties, and maintain high morals, although I do not believe in being strict at all. I guide my children and give them daily advice and teach them that there are limitations and difficulties to succumb and certain rules to follow so that they can cope better in life. I often mention to them "*You will never do anything in this world without courage and decency. These are the real qualities in life next to honor*".

There were enjoyable times too, when we all congregated at Mansur Club across from our house in Mansur City. There were many social gatherings and festivities held there with live music, movies shown in the special small movie theatres and banquets held in the vast gardens. My brother Alishan formed a band of his own and performed in this club. Men played cards and youth congregated in the community rooms.

Dancing with my father -"Hammurabi Gardens Restaurant" in Baghdad

The club also had a big pool and on the special days assigned to women, we would go swimming in the absence of male gender.

On hot summer days, we used to stroll at Zawra Park which was a large public garden full of people who came to pass time amidst the green lawns and colorful flower grounds. Families would take their children to the amusement park there or to visit Baghdad Zoo, one of the biggest in the Middle East. The place was alive with the voices of happy children in the public swimming pools where they cooled down.

This is a man's world as they have a lot of liberty. Monogamy is practiced and long gone are the days of polygamy. Men live a reputable life and stick to one woman to support her.

When visiting, it is advisable for women to go in groups and to be accompanied by a male, to dress sensibly and retain high standards.

"We are what we repeatedly do,
excellence then is not an act, but a habit." Aristotle

ART OF MYSTIC COFFEE GROUND READING – GAHWA

My own artwork – Leave a little magic wherever you go!

Magic Coffee

The art of coffee ground reading is very popular and widely practiced in Iraq. This is an ancient form of divination still unknown to the western world. An enjoyable experience in our lives is looking forward to drinking a cup of coffee, first for the taste, then for the excitement in discovering what shows in the grounds. Iraqi motto: *"Eat and drink always in an unhurried way."*

I have this natural gift and I have reached a new level in my life which has helped many people, as I predict the future with accuracy.

This innate ability reveals itself by one's intuitive skills and by tapping into one's unconscious mind and listening to your inner voice. This is an awareness which can be sharpened by your insight and the recognition of patterns which the grounds have formed in the cup and saucer, after the individual has consumed the coffee.

As a clairvoyant, it is a Higher Power which guides me together with presentiments. As a clairaudient, the auditory signals I hear simultaneously give me the ability to name people and events pertaining to the person's situation. I feel that I can breathe life into the coffee cup with intuitive faculties as I sense people's aura in a harmonious environment.

One masters the technique with practice, by listening extensively to their 'gut feeling' and thus it will become easy to relate to the person the significance of the pictorial representations.

So now you will value and enjoy your cup of coffee as I reveal a few facts about the life of the coffee tree.

The coffee plant grows on high plateaus beneath large shaded trees, several thousand feet above sea level. It self-pollinates. The beans flourish under the canopy of the rain forests and the many variations can be attributed to the water, soil and cultivation techniques.

My compassionate grandmother Azniv was the expert in the entire preparation from scratch. She bought the raw green coffee beans, roasted them in a large iron pan on medium fire. She watched closely as she constantly and patiently stirred the beans, and she would say: "*watch attentively as the color of the beans will magically change from green to brown.*"

I was curious as I observed the process and she then pointed out: "*keep an eye on the luster, never let the beans turn black so as to obtain a pleasant distinctive flavor without any bitterness.*" At this point the delightful aroma would drift all around the house, the courtyard and beyond to the neighbors who never missed a chance to eventually pop in and enjoy the freshest taste of the coffee.

She then spread the beans on large parchment paper sheets which would absorb the grease and allowed it to cool down in open-air. The process continued while she sifted the ingredients through a fine sieve and then poured the beans into a manual copper coffee grinder.

She would ask me to turn the handle several times and then stop to open the lower part of the grinder. Then she would say: "*the coffee is now pulverized; your hard work did pay off, and now smell the wonderful aroma.*" To this day, the fragrance still prevails and brings back nostalgic, appreciated moments as it was a time-honored tradition which I shall never forget.

Nowadays life is easier and all you have to do is to acquire a pound or two of finely ground coffee from a mid-eastern store. You need a demi-tasse, a coffee jug (jezve), water, sugar and coffee.

For two people add two cups of water, let it boil, then add two teaspoons of sugar and coffee. Stir and let the foam rise but be careful because it will spill over. Pour gently and voila', the magic works on its own.

After you drink the coffee, let the grounds sink to the bottom and allow to settle while it slightly dries, swirl the cup gently and turn it upside down in its saucer then let it rest for a few minutes.

The person's energy and thoughts are transmitted to the beverage which then transforms into images and relates to the subject's life. In quiet meditation, focus on the symbols and start the reading from the rim which pertains to the future, then the center which relates to the present and then the lower part which concerns to the past.

It is a fact that when I do the psychic readings, I feel that I am a channel for invisible forces, very keen to find solutions to people's lives. I can see in my mind's eye the meaning of these descriptive symbols incorporated with precise auditory signals. Words and names are whispered to me, which no one else can hear at that moment. I am then fully responsible to convey these messages to the subject.

As time goes by, the awareness and the power of observation intensifies and fortunately does not fade. With guidance, I manage to find solutions. The evidence lies in the testimonials I have from clients contained in a large number of diaries I have in my possession.

There are no secret codes to be taught, no special classes to attend, no books to turn to. This is purely a gift. So, if you have it, do not hesitate to use it. Ultimately there is "magic" in our coffee. As I was growing up, I came to realize that the pleasant black brew triggered alertness and warmth, while we as a family surrounded ourselves with friends.

The skeptics and non-believers need not be interested or curious because they would be wasting our time.

The paranormal skills in our family continue. I will always remember my grandmother Esther for her insights.

My mother Nevart on the other hand was very intuitive; she was endowed with extra sensory perception and had the natural ability to foresee upcoming events. Her dreams gave a sense of direction and readiness for what lay ahead. Visions and apparitions were the norm for her every day and she described them and recognized the entities as being benign, so we did listen to her predictions.

I also have to mention my daughter Sevan who is capable of seeing beings around in houses, who direct her path at all times. Her psychic experiences and insights are interesting, and we heed to them. Her instinctive sensitivity and sixth sense towards people and their lives is always credible. Her dreams also always have a meaning.

My son Manuel is a very kind and understanding soul, he also is sensitive and insightful as he can perceive the person's pure qualities and intentions and deep self-awareness with his social interaction with people.

So our family is gifted and we are forever grateful for it. Now YOU can develop your instinctive skills too, as you can tap into the forces and let your consciousness guide you.

"I trust my intuition to deliver inspiring visions of my future" Jonathan Lockwood Huie

If you are seeking answers in your life, just enjoy a delicious cup of mystical Armenian coffee and believe in its magic! Here are some images.

Figure 1-Roof   Figure 2-Parrot   Figure 3 -Airplane   Figure 8-Car

Figure 1 A new roof
Underneath is the outline of a face which means for you to be smart in your new endeavors, so that you can make better decisions in acquiring property.

Figure 2 - Parrot
The Parrot brings good luck and good news. Proceed with your plans but do not yet announce them to the world. Let the good times roll. Do not think about the past, the coffee grounds sliding downwards mean your worries will dissipate.

Figure 3 - Airplane
There's a trip ahead of you, a safe one. Well worth your time for a getaway, you will return with a different perspective and envision life differently.

Figure 4 - Angel
Profile of a protective angel with wings on left hand side, holding on to a gun. Believe in the power of angels around you. This one is going to take your troubles and danger away, have faith and be aware of your surroundings.

Figure 5-Shoe   Figure 6-Ship/Boat afloat   Figure 7-Profile of Bride   Figure 8-Car

Figure 5 -Shoe on left and a purse on the right
You will be facing problems with your feet. It is important to wear comfortable shoes without heels at all times. This also means poor circulation in your legs and feet. Purse, be careful where you place your purse-petty theft!

Figure 6 - A ship/boat afloat
You will be going on a trip by boat and the waters are clear beneath. Or follow the saying "Your ship is coming in".

Figure 7- Profile of a bride holding a bouquet of flowers.
There is a marriage ahead of you, union and then the birth of a child. A Very positive image.

Figure 8- Car.
Be careful how you drive. Be cautious on the streets. Back tire shows deterioration; have your engine checked frequently.

"Being Insightful, virtuous and honorable will allow you to access the voice within." My quote.

Some other meanings:

Dagger or sword: Arguments or disagreements – trouble ahead, do not make irrational decisions at this time.

Tree: Be steady and grounded without moving anywhere.

Flower: Joy and contentment, the fruits of your labor are satisfactory

Money Symbol: Financial improvement, success in business

Chair: Avoid delay, act fast and do not remain idle, wasting precious time not in your favor.

Book: Further learning possibilities which will lead to financial ease. Your present job not satisfactory but there is hope for improvement in the future.

Star: A wish fulfilled, successful times ahead.

Stork: Arrival of a child in your life, new addition to family

Tooth: Problems with your diet, teeth deteriorating, eat wholesome home-made food.

Two people facing each other: Business opportunities, venturing towards a new company with success.

Bottle: Drinking is in your disfavor, might cause accidents or you might get hurt on the roads and also damage your health.

Glass: Time to celebrate and recognize your talents coming to fruition

Bow or Arrow: Beware of false individuals – treachery and interference.

Car or airplane: A journey ahead

Half a heart: Domestic and romantic arguments and disappointments –Difficult undertaking- Failure or crisis in relationship

Bed: You will recover from an illness or successful surgery.

Pool of Water: Watch out when you are swimming, avoid deep waters.

Angel usually seen with wings: Good times ahead, you are protected, on the pursuit of a better standing in life. Financial ease.

Scissors: Remove your bad habits and tendencies, which might be hindering your life. Cut off the unnecessary patterns which are not working in your favor.

Musical Instrument: There will be harmony in your life, time be on the pursuit of happiness.

Clock: Be productive daily, do not procrastinate. Time is precious in your life.

Mountain: Time to focus on achieving your goal, since you have to climb up a mount to deserve success. Remaining inactive will make life worthless.

BREAKFAST IN THE CITY

Breakfast in Baghdad brings a favorite Iraqi breakfast cream 'Gaimar' to my mind. It is made from buffalo milk and turned into cream which is thick in consistency, and it is  sold mainly by the local Arab women from the suburbs of the city. Every morning, these women draped in long black abayas which covered them from head to toe, came to pay us a visit. They cleverly balanced circular trays on their heads in which lay a silver receptacle coated with this delicious cream and covered with thin white cheesecloth. It was very convenient to have this product sold at our doorstep.

These women arrived early morning. They were the suburban dairy farmers who milked and processed the product by hand from the buffaloes which would roam in the fields. To this date processing plants and factories cannot yield the same flavor that these women managed to produce. They also brought fresh yogurt.

They would gracefully set down the tray and with a knife slashed the cream in large triangles. It looked so rich yet it was mild in flavor with a fresh scent. We would then spread it on 'samoon' bread and pour honey or syrup on top. We had to consume it fresh because this product was not enhanced with any additives or preservatives and had a short shelf life.

The old-fashioned technique is still used by churning and boiling the milk for several hours then letting it cool down and slicing it. This process is time consuming and demands patience and expertise.

You could not help admiring the women's ivory gleaming white teeth. They would smile and tell you: "*No matter how often you brush your teeth, you will never see them sparkle, like our teeth, so if you have some of our gaimar or some of our yogurt, then you will see the difference*". We were convinced and sure enough, the results were evident.

For sustainable energy, mental awareness and better health, start off your day with a wholesome nutritious breakfast. It will give you a surge of energy and recharge your brain and body. It is considered to be the most important meal of the day! We also serve eggs, as well as olives, a variety of cheeses, butter and apricot jam, Foul salad (cooked fava beans mixed with tomatoes, parsley, and green onions. My favorite was 'Armenian Pancake', similar to crepes, on which we spread homemade apricot jam.

"All happiness depends on a leisurely breakfast" John Gunther

TEA – CHAI

An Iraqi cup of hot chai is appealing to everybody throughout the day. I remember the teapot brewing for several hours, just in case a visitor dropped by.

Several teahouses were spread throughout the city, mainly where men socialized as they sipped the dark perfected brew, played cards or backgammon and spoke of daily events.

Nowadays it is trendy to brew tea in a <u>double</u> boiler but on special occasions we would use the samovar. The double stacked kettles produced the tasty dark concentrate with a delightful strong aroma. Iraqis diligently prepare their cup of tea and you can also master the following technique.

1. Let water boil in the <u>lower</u> large kettle.
2. Add 2 tablespoons of loose tea leaves in the <u>upper</u> kettle and then pour the hot water over it. At this point, on lower fire, let it seep for at least twenty minutes so as to darken and reach a distinct flavor.
3. By using a strainer pour a small quantity of the concentrate from the upper kettle into small glasses called 'estikans', then dilute with boiling water and serve with cubes of sugar. To this hearty brew you could also add cinnamon or fresh mint to create a slightly different taste. We liked our tea strong and robust, with a distinctive character, but not bitter.

For those who wanted to add milk, we served tea in porcelain teacups as we wanted to maintain its appearance of dark amber, warm orange color and preserve its floral earthy brisk taste. We only used loose black tea leaves, which were kept in tightly closed jars in order to preserve the original taste. Iced tea was unheard of and tea bags were not used in Baghdad.

So what happens to the tea leaves in the cup? Well, they are added as a compost to enrich the soil. We do not have the habit of reading the pattern of the tea leaves, we leave that up to the Europeans. On the other hand, as mentioned before, we do read coffee grounds.

Only Iraqis have mastered the technique of pouring tea in a glass cup by separating the clear water from the dark brew. See it for yourself.

Even while shopping, the storekeeper would always be ready to offer you a cup of tea as a sign of gratitude, a 'good luck' omen he would say. Custom dictates that if there are more than two cups on a tray, you should choose the middle one. *"Strange how a teapot can represent at the same time the comforts of solitude and the pleasures of company"*.

HEARTY FLAVORS OF HOME - Let us
bestow our lavish hospitality to you.

The warm memories of aromas and flavors from our kitchen revive the recipes of my ancestors and create a legacy to my culture. Armenians cling to the past and our way of remembering our survival links us to the ongoing need to keep our long-established recipes alive.

I realize that practice makes one perfect and though these are not new creations I have slightly altered the ingredients to add a personal touch.

Every time I walk into the kitchen I am inspired by my childhood recollections as I reminisce the endless variety of delicious food on our table. I was taught daily to learn as much as I could just by watching attentively the step-by-step procedure given by my mother and grandmother. Culinary schools were unheard of so you had to learn at home, always in an unhurried way.

Although I was not interested when I was a teenager, I now feel that it would have been so much easier had I made more of an effort. But time makes a person wiser, so I now realize that it is important to delve into the precious old recipes as it is necessary to nourish the body, mind and soul with healthy homemade food. In Baghdad it was a pleasure to be in our fully equipped air-conditioned kitchen which had a well-stocked pantry with modern utensils, refrigerators and freezers.

"Why are our refrigerators and freezers always full?" I once asked my mother. The answer was *"to perceive plentitude and affluence and to keep scarcity and deprivation away from our homes. An empty refrigerator is like an empty soul."* I still believe in those words and feel it reflects a lot about one's personality A plenteous fridge is always satisfying, thereby leaving <u>no room</u> for poverty.

Today, I still consider it to be very important to be united during meals. The bond that is created brings us together and makes us understand life better, since it is a time to communicate and share the moments and memories of the day. Always setting up an attractive table with a nice presentation remains the norm of the day.

Hospitality in Iraq is unparalleled as it is a great pleasure to host guests at all times. Don't be surprised when Iraqis pile up your plate several times, since 'one helping' is never enough. And remember your table must have an immense visual appeal which will entice everyone's appetite. I remember everyone would stop and feast their eyes on the colorful medley of delicacies. So the 'eyes' must be fed first.

To this day, I feel it necessary to present a pleasant table setting. It is never too late to learn how to cook and these recipes are a staple of ours and easy to follow.

The final secret to the success of a recipe is to *"sprinkle a little bit of love into it, and, of course, the prime ingredient is patience"*, and remember, it is important to always develop good manners which says 'a lot about your character'.

It is a good sign to notice 'silence' at the table while eating. It means the food is delicious.

"Show gratitude every time you sit for a meal"

MEZZE - Mezze is a colorful medley of several appetizers served before the main course, accompanied with a glass of 'arak' – the anise flavored liquor for the adults or a glass of "Tann" the yogurt drink.

Jajeg-Yogurt Dip
2 cups of plain yogurt
1 cucumber diced
1 clove of garlic (optional)
2 teaspoons of dry crushed mint
A dash of salt
Pour yogurt in a bowl, add cucumbers and garlic. Mix in other ingredients.
(Secret –sprinkle fresh cut mint leaves over dip)

Potato Salad
4 Potatoes
½ bunch of scallions and 1 bunch of chopped fresh parsley
½ cup of olive oil
3 tablespoons of vinegar
Salt and pepper to taste

Boil potatoes, peel and cut in big slices. Sprinkle with parsley, onions, oil, vinegar, salt and white pepper.
(Secret: add the fresh juice of 2 lemons)

Hummus –Garbanzo Bean Dip
1 can of garbanzo beans
1 tablespoon of Tahini sauce
1 clove of garlic (optional)
1 tablespoon of olive oil - 2 lemons

Mix garbanzo beans, tahini sauce and ¼ cup water, lemon juice in blender. Then pour in separate dish and mix all ingredients. Decorate by pouring over hummus, the olive oil, olives, slices of tomato and red pepper.
(Secret Add 1 or 2 tablespoons of water if the sauce is too thick and a pinch of salt)

Foul Mudammas – Fava Bean Salad
1 can of Fava Beans
1 ripe sliced tomato, a bunch of parsley finely chopped, one garlic, a bunch of finely chopped scallions, ½ cup of olive oil, 2 freshly squeezed lemons, a teaspoon of vinegar. Mix all ingredients together and serve cold after one hour.
(Secret: Cook the beans beforehand for ten minutes before mixing in the ingredients)

Taboule' – Parsley Salad
¼ cup of 'Crushed Wheat' soaked in water then set aside
2 tomatoes diced
2 bunches parsley finely chopped
One bunch of Scallions finely sliced
3 freshly squeezed lemons
½ c olive oil
Salt and pepper
A dash of dry mint

Mix tomatoes, parsley, scallions, salt and pepper, and mint.
Drain crushed wheat and add to mixture. Pour lemon juice and olive oil. Place in refrigerator, Serve over a bed of Romaine lettuce leaves.
(Secret: add 1 teaspoon of red vinegar to add a tang to it)

Chicken tenders grilled served over salad

1 lb of chicken breast cut in cubes
2 tbs fresh squeezed lemon juice
½ tsp of oregano
2 tbsp of olive oil
½ tbs ground white pepper
2 crushed garlic cloves
1 sliced onion
¼ cup of tomato paste

Marinate chicken and set aside in fridge. After a few hours cook on a grill and serve in pita bread with mayonnaise and lettuce and tomatoes and sliced cucumber.
(Secret: add 2 tablespoons of yogurt to the marinade)

Lentil split pea soup

Chop the following ingredients
½ stick of butter
2 celery stalks
1 potato
2 carrots
1 onion – 2 cloves garlic
Half a bell pepper

Dry ingredients:
1 cup of split pea
½ cup of red lentil
¼ cup barley
Pour the above dry ingredients into 5 cups of water- set aside for 2 hours

Sauté all vegetables in butter-add 4 cups of water-let it cook for 20 minutes
Then add the second set of ingredients and over medium heat, cover pan with lid and let it cook for about 45 minutes. You will see the mixture thicken, so set on low fire for a few minutes. Place in blender to obtain smooth mixture and serve hot.
(Secret –add croutons for better results)

BOREK Puff Pastry Cheese Turnover
1 package of Puff Pastry frozen dough squares

One bunch of scallions cut in small pieces
1 cup Feta cheese
1 ½ cups Mozzarella skimmed cheese
One cup of chopped parsley
One cup of frozen spinach-optional (firmly squeeze out moisture)
Salt and white pepper

Preheat oven to 375 degrees
Combine ingredients in a bowl.
Scoop one rounded tablespoon of filling on dough
Fold by forming into a triangular shape, press the corners so that the stuffing does not ooze out.
Brush with whisked egg. Arrange on cookie sheet, place in oven until they turn golden brown.

Pasta - Sauce
Half stick of Margarine/Butter
1 Onion diced
2 fresh tomatoes and half green pepper diced
Two to three cloves of garlic
4 cups of broth
Salt, white pepper, oregano, red pepper,
4 tablespoons of tomato sauce and 1 teaspoon of sugar

Sauté onion, fresh tomatoes, garlic, salt, white pepper, oregano, red pepper
Add broth, cook for 20 minutes, add tomato sauce, and allow sauce to thicken
Mix in blender. Serve over pasta.
(Secret: Add Parmigiano Reggiano, 1 tablespoon of cream, 1 tablespoon of spreadable garlic cream cheese.)

Potato Curry Stew

1 lb stew meat beef
6 fresh mini potatoes
1 onion
1 garlic clove
4 cups broth - Salt, white and red pepper, pinch of all spice.

Cook meat in hot water until it is tender. Be attentive because you have to remove the scum that rises to the top. Then drain and set aside.
In a separate saucepan, add onion and garlic and saute' the meat for a few minutes. Then add the potatoes and blend with wooden spoon. Pour in broth and leave to cook for half an hour on medium fire. Then blend in curry powder. Cover saucepan. Let sauce thicken.

(Secret: Add the juice of two fresh lemons as a final touch and ½ teaspoon of starch.)

Rice Pilaf

1 cup of Basmati Organic Rice – washed and soaked for one hour
½ cup of vermicelli noodles
½ cup of corn oil – salt to taste
3 cups of chicken broth

Add oil to pan, let it heat slightly, then sprinkle the vermicelli noodles. Mix on low fire until it turns light golden brown. Drain rice and add to mixture, mix then pour over the broth and let it cook on medium fire until it absorbs all the liquid. Turn fire on low and taste to see if rice is cooked. Serve hot.
Secret: Mix in 1 teaspoon of butter. This renders the rice smoother to the taste.
During festivities we like to decorate the rice with the following:
Mix 1 cup of sliced almonds, 1 cup of white currants, a dash of 'all spice'. Pour some oil into a pan, add the almonds and continue mixing attentively until it turns golden, then add currants on low fire and continue mixing for another 10 minutes. Then add a teaspoon of "all spice" and mix for a few more minutes. Spread artistically over the rice.

THE NATIONAL MUSEUMS OF IRAQ - A GREAT CONTRIBUTION TO CIVILIZATION

When touring the National Museums in Iraq, it is exciting to learn about their rare collections of priceless relics and to develop awareness of the daily lives and customs of the ancient people of Mesopotamia.

You can venture into the halls and the galleries with guidebooks and admire the masterpiece exhibits. There are statues, alabaster vases, ceramic bowls, female and male figurines, detailed gold and silver jewelry, cylinder seals, pottery, manuscripts, mosaics, stone art and valuable historical collectibles.

The collection is carefully stored and displayed in well-lit glass showcases or placed on high pedestals. There is a great history to discover as one is transported back to the time of the Mesopotamian era, dating back 5,000 years, to a land populated by the Babylonians, Sumerians, Akkadians, Chaldeans, Assyrians and Seleucids.

The huge and impressive carved panels and murals once lined the walls of the palaces. The stone reliefs, plaques and tablets carry inscriptions conveying messages about civilization, the era when writing was first developed and the invention of the chariot wheel. These historical facts displayed are a true gift to humanity and contributed to progress and development.

The private collection of gold coins and ornate jewelry, amulets and headdresses depict an era of wealth and give an insight to the will power of a society ahead of their time in both art and culture.

In the museums the past cannot be obscured because visitors relate to their current lives by examining the objects left behind which still seem functional and practical. The preserved exhibits are informative and educational and encourage us to evolve and improve daily just as these people did. The Department of Antiquities is trying to attract more visitors as they strive to reclaim stolen treasures of a golden era, engaging in rendering this site as appealing as possible.

There also are other museums worth visiting. Baghdad National Museum, Baghdadi Wax Museum, Museum of National Costumes and Folklore, Museum of Popular Heritage, Museum of Iraqi Art, National Museum of Modern Art and the Museum of National History.

"So much of our future lies in preserving the past". Peter Westbrook

GERTRUDE BELL & BAGHDADI WAX MUSEUM

Gertrude Bell was a British archaeologist, traveler and author. During her frequent trips to Iraq, she fell in love with the Arabic language and culture. She was a brave diplomat and her competence and approach with the tribal leaders made her gain a great deal of respect. She soon became a political officer and was named 'Queen of the Desert'.

She became so infatuated, in fact, that she took part under the British mandate, to delineate the borders of the nation of Iraq with the assistance of Winston Churchill and T.E. Lawrence of Arabia. She also helped to establish a kingdom with the Hashemite dynasty and crowned Faisal in 1921 as King of Iraq.

She was the only courageous woman in the area interested in exploring the Babylonian ruins and during her daily expeditions to the sites, she discovered invaluable relics. Her excavations uncovered a valuable ancient past.

The skilled archaeologist believed that the rare collections excavated on this land had to remain in Iraq in order to safeguard the history of Mesopotamia. So the museum gained fame as hundreds of thousands of people developed interest and paid tribute to her achievements.

The several galleries leave an imprint of Iraq's past and depict scenes of ancient furniture. Traditional costumes and habits are depicted too. It also contains hundreds of paintings and thousands of books. Here the culture of Iraq and its customs and practices are preserved. The Baghdad Municipality is now in the phase of organizing the opening of a new museum which will showcase figures of monarchs and presidents and will also include personalities as Gertrude Bell who had helped shape this land. Her wishes of being remembered will finally come true.

Gertrude gained the mark of respect from the several tribes and sheiks as she learned and became fluent in the Arabic language and focused on increasing public interest and awareness worldwide. She took great pride in the making of a nation.

Her diaries, notes and correspondence show exceptional love and dedication to 'Mesopotamia' and are of great value as they contain material which still pertains to life in the Mid-East. We can benefit from and understand when analyzing the present situation there. She was a determined and diligent, hardworking woman. Her family believed in her and sent their resources to fund her program all for the interest of the Iraqi people.

Gertrude believed Iraq could become a stable modern state when she stated: "*The kingdom of Iraq has been placed on its feet and its frontiers defined, but its future, prosperity and progress rests with the <u>Iraqis</u> themselves. We shall, I trust, make it a great center for Arab civilization and prosperity.*" The underlying message "*future, prosperity and progress rests with the **<u>Iraqis themselves</u>***" means that our land needs no foreign conquerors or rulers to interfere in our policies.

The Baghdadi Wax Museum now houses several hundred wax figures and scenes of historical Iraqi people and their customs and costumes, rather than statues of famous personalities. It is situated by the Bab El Muatham. It is an interesting way of discovering the old Iraqi traditions and ways of life and a great resource of knowledge depicting the by-gone habits of the people. In this museum there is a plaque that commemorates Gertrude Bell's accomplishments and success in creating this establishment. Her picture is also posted on the walls of Shahbander Café'.

"I'm more a citizen of Baghdad than many a Baghdadi born and I will wager that no Baghdadi cares more for the beauty of the river or the palm groves, or clings more closely to the rights of citizenship which I have acquired!" Gertrude Bell

Gertrude would have been very proud to have known that 'The University of Mosul' is presently undertaking a great project of reopening King Ashurbanipal's Royal library with the cooperation of British Museum, UNESCO and international cultural organizations. It will be one of the greatest achievements in Iraq to revive and revitalize the knowledge of the kingdoms of Assyria. It will be a great repository of knowledge with the collection of ancient clay tablets, fragments, literary documents, chronicles in cuneiform script which have survived after the discoveries of British archaeologist Henry Layard.

Another archaeologist and novelist, Agatha Christie, had the occasion to visit the archaeological sites and was intrigued by the history of this land so she decided to write the famous novel *"They Came to Baghdad'* which ended up being a best seller. Whoever took a trip to this land, ended up loving the environment, its people and its history.

"We shall I trust, make it a great center of Arab
civilization and prosperity" Gertrude Bell

KHAN MERJAN

Khan Merjan was famous as a shelter for worldwide travelers. It was built in the 14th century and it accommodated merchants and traders. They would rest here before they proceeded with their caravans to their final destination on the Silk Road. The reason why the route leading to Khan Merjan was called the 'Silk Road' was because silk was the most precious commodity. It was transported along with gems, gold, silver, fruit, aromatics, carpets, and precious fabrics.

It maintains its old charm and still preserves its authenticity. The large courtyard is now a restaurant, was once a place where people and their animals were tended to. It was also where merchants would have their merchandise stored away safely and where the caravans would rest for a few days.

This structure was bustling with business and it gained fame as travelers reached the height of their prosperity. There was an exchange of merchandise and while the east got acquainted with the west, people of all nations acted in solidarity with each other. Regardless of race, origin or religion, this was where trade was encouraged. The people had one common goal and that was to reach a mutual benefit in the business world.

A large portico gate leads to the main hall which is roughly 50 ft. high and is surrounded by arches laid out in brick. The windows are stained colored glass and shed rays of light on the environment. There are also niches for better air circulation. For the safety of everyone, in the early days, several guards were stationed at the entrance main door.

Khan Murjan has been renovated. The original courtyard is covered by several arches and domes which are pleasantly lit at night. The wooden stairs lead to the second floor which has several rooms surrounded by a gallery and bordered by a balcony. In the large fully air-conditioned dining room, the waiters all wear the traditional 'Saya' covered with a cloak. They are cordial and attentive and speak the real Iraqi Arabic language. In the evenings, folk musicians provide entertainment and famous Iraqi vocalists bring joy to the crowd.

The food is truly authentic Iraqi too. Starting with mezzes, then the main entrée, followed by dessert and coffee. Local beer accompanies the food, either 'Florida' brand or 'Diana' in addition to Arak Mestaki, the anise flavored liquor. In the side chambers only men are seen busy talking and smoking their 'nargile'.

This historical inn offers fascinating stories too. It is said that paranormal activities have taken place here. At times innkeepers and guests have seen lights flicker; visions of supernatural shadowy figures manifest themselves, and echoes of mumbling sounds emanate from the second floor. Brisk footsteps echoing through the various corridors, floors creaking have been heard coming from the rooms, and side doors swinging open.

I imagine that the presence of their lingering spirits and energy left behind demonstrate their desire to express that there is still a profound sense of successful activity going on. Long ago, tradesmen flourished, and merchants made fortunes at this spot. Thus, it is good to believe that prosperity and beneficial business success might be coming your way. This mystery is to be discovered by all those who will visit the caravanserai for sheer good luck.

"Fortune favors the prepared mind" Louis Pasteur.

Photo courtesy of Zaidoun Gabar (famous vocalist & musician in Iraq) with his wife Shahd Mudhafar

Many statues in Baghdad have a connection to the 1,001 Arabian Nights Tales.

Facing the Tigris River stands the famous statues of Princess Shehrezade and Prince Sharyar at Abu Nawass Street.

They were created by Mohammed Ghani who decided to make this Princess come to life and relive the legendary 1,001 Arabian Night tales.

Shehrezade stands proudly in front of the prince who is reclining yet listening attentively to her. She has a smile on her face and she conveys strength and reasoning, persuasiveness and pride with the gesture of her hands. Her long hair flows down her back and the long robe she wears portrays a woman of elegance and pride.

This bronze sculpture stands on the riverfront with a story for everyone; it is a fascinating tale of the intelligent storyteller who uses her common sense to stay alive by narrating her stories.

Prince Shahryar does not look antagonistic, nor does he express resentment. He shows curiosity as she has tamed his anger and has captivated him with her beauty and power of her intelligence.

The tales of 1,001 Nights are entertaining and amusing. They have a Middle Eastern flavor and one can acquire a lot of knowledge about the culture and the life of people during the period of Harun El Rashid.

This story is about King Sharyar who is very disappointed with his first wife when he finds out that she has been deceitful and consequently he puts an end to her life. He also forms a personal opinion that women are not to be trusted thereby he decides to get married several times and after the first wedding night, he puts an end to their lives.

The people of the city are appalled by his behavior but do not have the courage to rebel or stop him.

One day the sultan's daughter Shehrezade, who is very beautiful and intelligent, comes to hear about these sad events and she immediately decides to concoct a plan to stop his wrongdoings.

She visits the palace with her sister and introduces herself to him. Prince Sharyar is mesmerized by the way she presents herself boldly and decides that this is a woman he should marry.

The marriage takes place, and her plan commences. The night of the marriage, she sits in front of him and begins to recount several stories, captivating the prince's attention as he finds them to be fascinating and imaginative. She is determined to survive and in a very clever manner she stops narrating when the clock strikes midnight, telling him she is tired and will continue the next day.

Consequently, the Prince is fascinated by her charm and shows great interest to hear the rest of the story.

Her intelligent technique works and his outlook of life changes. His anger diffuses and his love for her intensifies daily. She witnesses his transition and in turn he spares her life while continuing to cherish her. He also manages to control his resentment towards women.

The underlying message here is that women have the skill and ability to use logic to have a positive effect on men. Especially those who go through a process of unreasonable anger which can be harmful not only to them, but also to loved ones around them.

"For all things difficult to acquire, the intelligent person works with perseverance". Lau Tzu

NOSTALGIA ALONG ABU NAWASS STREET – FAMOUS FOR FISH 'MASGOUF'

بغداد الحلوة بالليل

"We must begin to think like a river if we are to leave a legacy of beauty and life for future generations". David Brower.

Abu Nawass was the most famous street in the capital. It stretched for three miles along the mighty Tigris River and had well maintained parks, green lawns with multicolored flowers in addition to evergreen eucalyptus and palm trees. The gift of alluvial silt which deposits magically turned everything colorful with artfully planted flowers and plants which emanated a sweet fragrance in the air.

Two bronze statues on this street are now famous landmarks. The first sculpture is of the nationalistic poet 'Abu Nawass' by Ismael Fattah and the second is 'Shehrezade and Shahriyar' by Mohammed Ghani Hikmet.

When the sun set down its flaming rays, we loved to stroll along the riverside. We would enjoy the view of colorful string lights glistening in the water, the steady rhythm of the sailing boats (ballams) peacefully drifting by and the array of families and couples walking along the esplanade. Everyone here was simply seeking a break from the day.

The outdoor cafeterias, restaurants, first class hotels, pool halls, ice cream parlors and casinos were a delight for everyone. The street would be alive, filled with locals and tourists with music humming from the eateries. Alongside the roads were many art galleries exhibiting the works of various well-known Iraqi artists and sculptors which attracted a lot of visitors from the Arabian Peninsula.

This was an affluent area where all the embassies and consulates were built, where tourism was thriving and everyone came to eat the traditional fish dish 'Masgouf.'

Just before we reached this area, from afar, we would see pockets of bonfires burning; this was our destination. The open-air eateries lined along the riverfront and as we got closer we could smell the delicate scent of fresh fish wafting through the air.

"Shabbout" was the Mesopotamian freshwater carp, flavored with salt, spices and lemon and basted with a special marinade and oil. It was then placed on four wooden stakes which were pinned to the ground all around the burning fire.

The heat from the flames and embers roasted the fish slowly and added a slightly smoked flavor while retaining its moisture. The flesh would become firm and juicy with a glossy appearance yet crispy on the outside.

Adding the final touch, it was served with flatbread, salad and pickled spicy mango slices called 'amba'. No matter which country you go to, or however you cook this fish, it will never taste the same as it did along the Tigris. It is also said that many heads of states and foreign delegations, including Jacques Chirac of France visited, and appreciated this dining experience.

After consuming 'masgouf' it was time for dessert and coffee. We would go to the Italian cafe' where they had introduced various flavors of soft-serve ice cream, called 'Merry Cream', my favorite being vanilla. It was something new for the Iraqis and very much enjoyed, becoming so popular that people waited in long lines to consume the delightful treat. Then it was time to go and buy delicious, freshly fried potato chips to take home. They were found sizzling on the immense frying electric pans from the stores which served only this item.

As time went by, foreign businesses started booming here. On certain nights we went to the hotels and sat on their verandas overlooking the river and would listen to a band play, whilst eating and dancing the night away. The Palm Beach and Ambassador Hotels are now the most popular alongside the riverfront.

Even if you went just to sit on the benches, in a relaxed atmosphere, you would appreciate the steady rhythm of the boats cruising by, sending echoes of music and singing all along the river course. These were families playing the 'oud', drums and tambourines, and singing well- known Iraqi songs as they rifted by along the river of happiness which enhanced the pleasure of the evening.

My Family Photo Dining At Abu Nawass 1958   Linda Ohanian Dining at Abu Nawass
Riverfront-Baghdad 2017

This mighty ancient Tigris River, which sustained civilizations still glides swiftly, undisturbed from daily circumstances as it fulfills its task and helps the landscape around the shores remain lush and green. It did not bother me to see the water always murky, never transparent or crystal clear, because it had the power to replenish the plains abundantly with vegetation.

Our front and back yards were always green because the waters contained a high level of silt and minerals which even on the hottest days, was sufficient to render best results.

The river seemed to breathe new life into our land whilst it flowed smoothly and silently it would sweep its troubles and sufferings far away to discharge into its final destination, the Shatt el Arab. I compare it to life because without constant movement and progress, life would stagnate.

"O blessed Tigris I greet your banks from afar, oft have I been forced to drink from springs which did not my thirst quench".

Mohammed Mahdi al-Jawahiri

AL FAW PALACE –

The Faw Palace stands a few miles away from the international airport, yearning for tourists and visitors as its popularity increases daily.

Would you like to book a room in one of the grandiose Baghdad palaces along the outskirts of the capital city? A very pleasant spot amidst a vast clear blue lake, surrounded with lush healthy palm trees.

The presidential palace was a recreation spot used exclusively by government officials and their family members for weekend pleasures, hunting and fishing.

The colossal entrance doors lead to the rotunda flanked by several marble columns. At the center, on the high ceiling hangs a huge crystal chandelier which glimmers and sparks the light onto the marble floors. The room is surrounded with stairways leading to balconies around the hall with gilded ornate arched entries.

The palace has sixty rooms and 30 bathrooms with gold fittings and fixtures, several ballrooms, conference rooms and banquet rooms. The ceilings have carved reliefs with colorful paintings illustrating the recapture of the city in southern Iraq.

At the entrance there is a majestic throne which was a present from Yasser Arafat. It is made out of lacquered wood and the images on the chair illustrate the Dome of the Rock in Jerusalem, with the script *"Jerusalem is ours"*. Arafat's headscarf blueprint is illustrated and the verses from the Holy Quran read: *"In the name of God, the merciful and gracious, glorifies who traveled his servant by night from Mecca to Jerusalem"*. On the arch of the chair is written *"Victory from God and conquest is soon"*.

Right next to the throne is a colossal copper coffee pot. It depicts grandeur and is alleged to be the tallest coffee pot in existence. It symbolizes hospitality and a welcoming emblem to the people.

From the balconies one would admire the azure clear pond full of carp, catfish and bass. Motorboats were used to cruise around and reach the complex of Mediterranean villas built around the lake.

This was a favorite spot for elite professional anglers who would come during the weekends and aim to catch the important fish called' Saddam's Bass', chosen for its gleaming gold diamond scales and fins.

The innumerable cellars underground contained wines from all over the world especially chosen to be served with these fish delicacies during meals.

The palace was built in the 1990's to honor the Iraqi soldiers who freed the Al Faw Peninsula in southern Iraq in 1988 and regained it from the Iranians. The walls bear witness as the reliefs in Arabic give victory and glory to the combatants for their bravery in liberating their city.

At night, the fountains reflected multicolor lights as water flowed and spouted in the air making the spot look like a magical place in the splendor of 1,001 Nights. The once upon a time unapproachable palace is now open to the public who are in amazement of the grandeur they see. *"Enjoy present pleasures in such a way as not to injure future ones."* Seneca

Saddam Hussein decided one day to embellish the landscape, so he added a tiny island which you can see in front of his palace. He loved Date Palms and had them planted in order to enjoy his favorite dates. He regarded the tree as being protective, resistant, tolerant and sturdy enough to live up to a century. Did it describe his aspiration? Maybe a remedy to his wellbeing. The ancient fruit of civilization connected him to Babylonians, who believed in good fortune by these trees, to ward off evil energy. So he took great pleasure in observing the clumps of fruit grow and mature and looked forward to enjoying its nutritional values to keep him well-nourished and energized. One important factor was that no one else could enjoy the fruit from this tree except for him.

Dates in fact are antioxidants and contain fiber and promote brain health, remedy for diabetes because they are naturally sweet. Combine with walnuts, pistachios, or almonds and enjoy the wonderful taste. Dates are one of the most important export commodities of this land.

AL SHAHEED MONUMENT

An enormous eternal flame burns continuously under the shadows of the two split ceramic turquoise tile dome shells at the Shaheed Monument in Baghdad.

It is called the "Marty's Monument" and is of national significance to commemorate the brave fallen soldiers of the Iraq/Iran war.

The site is visited by many, including foreign dignitaries, to honor and show gratitude for the soldiers' sacrifice. The structure is built in the middle of an artificial lake with water which cascades to the lower floors. It stands 110 feet high and underneath the domes there was a cafeteria, a museum, a library, exhibition room and art gallery.

The parks and playgrounds as well as the walkways which surround the lake make for a memorable day. Every year ceremonies are held by government officials and visiting international heads of other states. This monument was erected in 1983 and it is customary to allow yourself ample time during your visit as this trip will provide you with a daily appreciation of life

"Peace means far more than the opposite of war" Fred Rogers

THE UNKNOWN SOLDIER MONUMENT

This colossal monument was built to honor the fallen soldiers, it commemorates their sacrifice during the Iran/Iraq war. Remains of unidentified soldiers were buried here.

This high-profile landmark has a round dome which symbolizes a shield plunging to the ground from the hands of an unseen dying soldier. It appears inclined in mid-air over an eternal flame which burns in a steel cube.

The cube is built in seven layers representing 'the seven layers of Heaven' from the Holy Qur'an. An ulterior set of three red sheets amongst the layers represents the vital force of fallen soldiers.

Next to it is a spiral flagpole made up entirely of panels made with glass imported from Murano Italy, the undisturbed island on the Venetian Lagoon. It is known worldwide for the production of the finest enduring colored glass, which does not fade under the exposure of the sun and maintains its brilliance under any type of weather. So famous is the glass blowing technique and so highly esteemed, that the Italian glass makers were not allowed to leave the island for fear their secrets would be exposed to the outside world.

The monument is fully lit at night by floodlights. It is built in the form of a circular ziggurat with three colored panels in green, white and black representing the colors of the national flag saluting the dead soldiers.

No one remains unknown to God and the soldiers' families and this monument gives a compelling message as to how <u>SENSELESS a war can be.</u>

The staircases led to an underground museum which used to store war relics but is now empty. The impact of the shafts of light filtering through the upper openings and doors is striking, as the rays of the sun illuminate the center of the whole chamber like God's light shining upon the soldiers' souls.

Memorial Day is celebrated at this site every year. When heads of states visit Iraq, they are always accompanied by a big parade of military personnel to honor and pay tribute to the soldiers while they place colorful wreaths at the site, leaving a melancholy reminder of an unnecessary war.

"Whoever recommends and helps a good cause becomes a partner therein, and whoever recommends and helps an evil cause, shares its burdens." Holy Qur'an 4:85

MUSTANSARIYA UNIVERSITY

Mustansariya is the "palace of wisdom' and stands majestically overlooking the Tigris River.

This was the center of learning and culture, where scholars studied and translated worldwide languages such as Greek, Syrian and Persian. In addition, Indian literary scripts were later added to their daily curriculum.

Ancient texts were introduced and studied in order to broaden the worldwide awareness to the student. This was a 'madrassa', a school set up for learning Arabic theology, sciences, medicine and mathematics. It also contained a large library and an astronomical and scientific observatory.

The institution was built by Caliph El Mustansariyah in 1228. Its architecture includes a series of ornate embellished arches which open up to a courtyard where a large fountain still stands. The vaulted corridors and halls lead to the prayer rooms and living quarters for the scholars.

The styles on the ornate entrance door as well as façade and arcades are decorated with geometrical and floral arabesque designs. The brickwork molded in plaster is symmetrically carved in layers on the inner part of the arches.

Caliph Mustansariyah yearned to make life more pleasant and picturesque for the scholars. He added beauty to the grandeur by having large parks, lush ponds and a grandiose garden built along the riverside. He said "*I chose this site for its delightful gardens so that you may be able to enjoy the view of the unhindered flow of the Tigris River*". It was a perfect spot as the waterway system irrigated the area and yielded a beautiful panorama which somehow encouraged and brought hope, as well as a desire for the students to continue to maintain a love for education.

During the year 1258, when the Mongols invaded the city, they wanted to erase any form of educative material and install their own decrees. They ransacked the institution and hurled as many volumes and manuscripts as they could into the river.

It was said that the Tigris turned black from the ink of the books. Fortunately, a large number of documents were hidden in vaulted underground rooms, thereby eventually saved.

"Knowledge is Power" Sir Francis Drake

Two holy cities of worship stand near each other. These are destination points for Muslims throughout the world. Waves of pilgrims journey to these cities to experience religious renewal.

In Kerbala they commemorate the anniversary of the deaths of Imam Hussein, Imam Abbas and the seventy-two other martyrs who were assassinated during the Battle of Tuff 1,400 years ago.

It is a holy observance and the devout take this trip at least once in their lifetime, carrying out sacred rituals to pay homage to the pain and suffering of the Imams. Worshippers come here to become obedient to Allah and to stay away from vice and sins. To become righteous, they humble themselves by flogging their body as they ask for miracles.

In Kerbala, at Al Husseiniya mausoleum, lies the tomb of Imam Hussein who was the grandson of the Prophet Mohammed. It is made of marble and the sarcophagus is decorated with ivory and enamel, surrounded by a high silver fence decorated in gold. It has a gold dome and two gold minarets.

The interior of the shrine is fully carpeted and richly embellished with thousands of mirrors, mosaic crystals, silver and gold gemstones. Older people come to this mausoleum with the firm intention of being buried here one day, as they believe, according to the Holy Qur'an, that the gates here open to paradise.

When you visit either Kerbala or Najaf you become a Haj (male) or Hajji (female) which is a term added to your name as a form of respect.

One of the important sayings in the Holy Qur'an is that *"on the day of resurrection, your eyes, ears and heart are the best witness of what you have done during your lifetime"*.

Kerbala also covers an area where the soil is extremely fertile and water is plentiful thus the best tasting fruit is grown here. Orchards and palm groves yield the sweetest and most delicious fruits.

Najaf is where Ali Ibn Talib is buried. He was the son in law and cousin of Prophet Mohammed and he is honored as a martyr.

Millions of pilgrims also visit His sarcophagus which is placed in a rectangular enclosure in this mosque.

The large dome and two minarets are overlaid with gold tiles and the neon lights, mirrored walls and precious stones.

Najaf is also very famous and people who visit Kerbala make it a point to walk from one house of worship to the other as a form of respect.

Here lies the largest cemetery where famous prophets are buried. It is called the 'Valley of Peace', and Muslims aspire to be buried at this site. Theologists and scholars who study religion go to Najaf also as it is famous for its many schools of Muslim faith.

This is the burial site of Imam Ali who was one of the most important caliphs. He was known as the originator of the Shia credence so thousands of pilgrims from all over the world visit this holy site.

The holy shrine is found in the center of the city and reflects beautiful Islamic architectural art and design.

The entrance leads to a large courtyard, has 58 halls and in each one there stands the sarcophagus of renowned Islamic religious leaders.

Ali's tomb is square and is enriched with valuable-colored marbles, mirrors, crystals and mosaics. The holy grave is covered with mahogany and ivory in arabesque style. Steel and silver fences also surround the tomb for safety purposes. Frequently seminars are held to enrich the knowledge of the Islamic beliefs.

Many gold items have been set with diamonds and rubies and gold crowns. Jewels with emeralds and priceless pearls adornments of precious stones surround the halls. Gold and silver swords are displayed on the walls. Embroidered window coverings made with gold and silver thread as well as precious carpets adorn the chambers. Valuable documents written from the Holy Qur'an are also preserved here.

I believe it is important to mention the famous quotes of Imam Ali which to-date are worthy to be taken into consideration:

"You humans, think that you are insignificant, while there is a great universe contained in you" - "Adversities often bring good qualities to the front" - "When few blessings come your way, do not drive them away through ungratefulness" - "If you get opportunity and power over your enemies, then in thankfulness, forgive them" - "A wise man first thinks then speaks and a fool speaks and then thinks".

ZUMURRUD KHATOUN

Zumurrud Khatoun was the cousin and wife of Abbasid Caliph Harun El Rashid, and became a famous princess. Her husband, who was an ingenious man, was the fifth Abbasid Caliph who founded a library known as the 'house of wisdom'.

The ornate mausoleum in Baghdad was built in 1201 A.D.in her honor. She was a woman of great intelligence and power, courageous, kind and beautiful. She was also interested in literature and science. Many scholars and dignitaries came from other countries to see her so as to gain insight about numerous civilizations.

Zubaida was an important individual who gave counsel to her husband and amazed the elite during his reign. During his military expeditions, she took charge of the kingdom.

There exists a road called 'Zubaida's Route' and also another waterway called 'Zubaida's River' both in connection to her generosity.

On her first visit to Haj, she observed the path the pilgrims were taking, the toil and the sufferance in the heat and the thirst they endured to reach their destination from Baghdad to Mecca. She had to render their voyage easier. These were dedicated devout people whose journey had to become easier.

So when she returned to her kingdom, she set up a plan to provide an aqueduct, a number of wells and reservoirs to provide clean and healthy drinking water for the pilgrims.

This act of compassion and benevolence was recognized by many, so the memory had to continue to live on.

So here is the tomb of the Princess, which is of Arabian architecture, composed in a design resembling beehive shaped combs in nine layers on a minaret. It rests on an octagonal base with holes which allow the light to filter through to the interior vault and is topped with a cupola.

The reason for the shape of the structure was to protect the site from winds, the hot sun and the rain. The sizzling air in the summertime would float upwards and allow the lower floor to remain cooler.

The Princess kept herself busy as a bee and employed attendants to accompany her to the site to recite and memorize the Holy Qur'an. They say a busy humming sound was heard at a certain time of the day which indicated that they were all praying at that time.

This is Sheikh Omar Mosque built similar to Zumurrud khatoun tomb

From this we can understand the link to the style this tomb was built. It denotes her will and desire to keep herself fully occupied and committed, with a purpose in life.

*"In life, the flow of time has
to be beneficial"*.

SOUK EL SAFAFIR-COPPER MARKET

The luster of the copper ornaments which decorated the shelves added a warm glow to our homes.

It is a different shopping experience which takes us to 'Souk el Safafir' This copper market is situated amidst a labyrinth of little stores in the alleyways located at the center of Baghdad.

The echoes of coordinated pounding sounds are heard from afar and as one approaches the area, one can't help but admire the work of art by the coppersmiths, ambitious craftsmen busy at work.

They sit in front of their stores and cut a strip of copper, heat it, bend it and twist it. Since copper is malleable and soft, they then shape and carve it with engraved designs by means of their etching tools.

Each strike on the copper is meaningful to the alert artisan as he painstakingly creates an everlasting metal art piece. He shows dedication and a strong will as he uses the traditional century old techniques involving hammers, mallets and old implements which are still in existence.

In a modern era, this is admirable; as the little stores all huddled together have a vast collection of polished decorative art, ready to embellish our homes. Since these gleaming ornaments are handcrafted, the slight imperfections make them unique and valuable. In the maze of innumerable number of small stores, many copper items are displayed on their shelves.

The coppersmiths show ambition in their work as well as motivation in devoting their time to an art which will always be appreciated.

They are self-disciplined and with intense concentration and focus, they create these objects and when asked about their skill, they modestly say *"with practice, experience, eagerness and patience, we strive for excellence"*.

This is admirable, because either 'rain or shine', through intense heat or severe cold weather, they continue their trade without complaints.

Copper bracelets were in fashion too, as it was believed that it was a real remedy for arthritis and pain in the bones. The copper would be absorbed through the skin and act as an anti-inflammatory agent and would also act as a remedy to anemia.

Copper does not age, it just tarnishes, but with a cloth and a few strokes, it once again revives its gold color and maintains its gleaming shine.

"The daily grind of hard work gets a person polished".

SPICE MARKETS BAHARAT

This market conjures up images of the ancient spice caravan routes which played a major role in the development of this country.

In fact, the flow of merchandise travelling to Ctesiphon through the Arabian Deserts created the age of discovery of spices. Arab merchants took over the trade and they used the rivers Tigris and Euphrates as a means to transport newly discovered herbs for food and medicinal purposes.

The only link to the past is to enjoy the 'Spice Market' which is filled with all kinds of rare new spices and herbs readily available.

The air is very heavy with exotic aromas when approaching the open-air marketplace. Kiosks are built side by side with numerous assortments of rows of sacks and barrels overfilled with vibrant multicolored spices.

It is a pretty sight for the visitor and so different than other countries where only small spice jars are sold.

Not much effort is needed in choosing from the assortment which includes saffron, dill, thyme, dry lime, mint, cumin, curry, nutmeg, frankincense, myrrh, chamomile, sumac and so much more.

The vendor usually also proclaims that he has the best domestic and foreign products together with natural ingredients to cure certain ailments. They ask you about your symptoms and accordingly prepare and grind the remedy drug manually, on the spot, which usually gives positive and beneficial results. Many people turn to these non-conventional drugs which leave neither side effects nor discomfort.

The 'herbalists' are health professionals who advise the benefits from these herbs which can bring relief from the symptoms and are safe to use. Drug stores were first launched in Baghdad around 754 A.D. and the practice continues with a mission to improve your health.

Here are some examples: Za'atar: an antiseptic, stimulates the brain and improves memory. You will feel motivated after you dip some bread into a plate full of olive oil and za'atar.

Dry Lime: cut into pieces, boil in 5 cups of water. The brew will darken in fifteen minutes, pass through a sieve, add a teaspoon of honey and drink periodically during the night- it will ease stomach aches and you will feel rested.

Chamomile flowers: boil 2 cups of water then add 5 teaspoons of chamomile flowers, let it boil on low fire and then let it rest for 10 minutes. Drain then add sugar and fresh lemon juice. This will help with your digestion and will relax the nerves and help you sleep.

Anise: aromatic taste. -You can also chew it to eliminate bad breath, added to liquor to enhance and create a delicious popular drink called 'Arak'. Great for stomach problems and toothaches. Rub your gums to alleviate pain as it numbs the area.

Pulverized coffee: if you start bleeding, quickly spread coffee sparingly over wound, it will stop the bleeding.

"Nature is my medicine". Sara Moss

BLESSED MOTHER ARMENIAN CHURCH-MESKENTA

Here they come to seek miracles

In Baghdad we had religious freedom and we could practice our Christian faith.

We attended the Blessed Mother Church which represented divine motherhood. It is situated off Rashid Street in Midaan Square in Baghdad. It was built in the 1640's and reconstructed in 1960's. It is hidden behind winding alleys, in the older part of the capital and concealed from the main roads. However it is so well known that anyone can guide you to the site.

Upon entering this church, I would feel a spiritual solace which would overpower me as I watched the numerous people praying and believing in the sanctity of the Holy Mother. The religious center was small and compact, plain and simple. One felt a sense of peace whilst glancing at the image in front of the simple demure altar devoid of fancy icons and decoration.

Known as the 'Church of Miracles Meskenta' it is particularly famous because it features a sacred metal chain enshrined on the wall by the altar. Upon your request, the priest placed the chain around your neck, fastened it and said a prayer and then you are asked to make a silent wish. If the chain got undone by itself, your wish would come true, if not, then it did not.

Throughout the year people bring their offerings in true faith believing that a miracle will be given by the Blessed Mother. Women who desired to be blessed with a child or had a sick member of the family would bring a blanket, spread it on the ground and pray and meditate until dawn.

On the day of Ascension, the 15th of August, a special mass takes place several times during the day and the devout overcrowd the church as many people had previously experienced miracles here.

The 'Church of Graces' is a place where Armenians sought refuge after the genocide. They came in droves, famine stricken, searching for survival and peace and in this place, they were granted the opportunity. The church was built in the name of Kevork Nazarian by order of the Ottoman Governor of Baghdad known as Gog Nazar.

Kevork Nazarian was an Armenian Military Officer who pursued the idea of building immense fortified walls circling the city to protect it against invaders. Because of his wisdom, the city remained safe and never fell into the enemy's hands. Due to this endeavor, he was recognized by the Sultan and granted the right to obtain a piece of land on which to build a church.

There is another true story linked to this place, about a building inspector who wanted to demolish the church and upgrade the commercial area surrounding it. The same night of his visit, the inspector experienced an overwhelming dream. He heard a deep voice say out loud *"Whoever demolishes this church shall perish"*. This dream was so vivid and clear, so frightening and real that he immediately woke up, shaken with a clear image of his experience. For several days, he was distressed and troubled and restless up to the point of not being able to sleep at night from the fear of another vivid dream.

He was convinced that he had to act immediately. Not knowing if all this was really happening to him and trying to reach an explanation, he contacted all his staff and narrated the dream. Upon seeing the alarmed and astounded reaction of his people, he finally decided to put an end to the project.

In pursuit of miracles, the church still stands. Another Armenian Orthodox Church in Al-Jadiriya is considered a top-rated attraction in the capital. The Armenians were the first to adopt Christianity in 301 A.D., evangelized by the apostles Bartholomew and Thaddeus. The Kingdom of Armenia, including King Tiridates III and his court, converted to this religion by Gregory the Illuminator.

While on this subject, I have to associate a great place of interest in Italy we used to visit which was the wonderful Basilica of 'Madonna di Fontanellato' about 14 miles from Parma. This Dominican monastery is famous as the 'Lady of the Rosary' continues to work her power. You walk through the chambers and galleries and marvel at the collection of thousands of exhibits and testimonies that adorn the walls and still bear strong witness of the performance of miracles. At the altar, the Blessed Mother stands with Jesus in her left hand and a rosary with a rose tied to her right hand. She peacefully waits to greet people and grant them their wish. I make it a point to honor her every time I am in Italy.

I have her artwork in my home and at night I kneel and say my prayers. While I meditate and I focus on her image, if it is to be granted, I surprisingly see the shadow of a luminous flashing glow around the frame on the wall. It is a sign that I have been heard and thus this gives me a great sense of strength and confidence.

"Somewhere right now, a miracle is happening."

SWORDS OF QUADDASSIYAH – VICTORY HANDS

The gigantic, crossed swords, forming a triumphal arch, lead you to the parade grounds and festival square In Baghdad. This is where many celebratory processions, floats as

well as flamboyant festive displays took place. A ceremonial march followed by military parades. Dignitaries and important government officials observed the show from a large pavilion built in the center of the grounds. The president and his elite would begin the ceremony while entering the scene on white horses.

The fists holding the Swords of Qadassiyah, which are seen rising from the ground, are an actual replica of Saddam Hussein's arms and hands. They are hollow inside and one can climb into these fists, while the blades are said to be cast from the melted armaments of deceased Iraqi soldiers. The nets below each arch contained the helmets of Iranian soldiers gathered from the battleground.

The swords of Quadassiyah were first unveiled in 1989 and were built to commemorate the victory of Iraq during the Iran Iraq war. This monument thereby has a connection to the glorification of the Quadassiyah Battle in 637 A.D. where the Persian Sassanian armies were defeated by the Arabian forces. A victorious campaign took place and marked the end of the Persian Sassanid Empire.

This monument has not been dismantled or destroyed and will be preserved for its historical value. One cannot bring the past alive but the sculptured forearms and fist of the late president still physically exist only here. Although the scene renders a solemn experience and a sentiment of sorrow it gives a clear message. *"The power of a gun is short lived" Dalai Lama*

Once you cross the drawn-out shadow of the swords, you cannot fail to be mindful that the whole world sees the misfortune that lies in the blades and the nets. It will be a constant reminder that peace and freedom do overall prevail.

"If the enemy inclines towards peace, do thou (also)
incline towards peace" Holy Qur'an 8:61

FLAT ROOFTOPS OF BAGHDAD - "Every Sunset brings a promise of a new dawn" Ralph Waldo Emerson

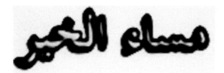

"When you sleep in a house your thoughts are as high as the ceiling, when you sleep outside, they are as high as the stars" Bedouin Proverb.

Along came summer and the sweltering heat. So we would head to our flat rooftops, our summer quarters during the hot season and the only place we could rest in the open-air with the hope of catching the faintest breeze. This tradition still lives on.

As dusk fell and it got dark, we hastened to prepare the beds. We unrolled the comforters and white sheets. These were kept rolled because we did not want the intense sun to bleach the colors. Grandma Azniv used to tell me *"Let's slightly sprinkle the sheets with cold water"*. I looked at her puzzled, whilst she uttered *"you will feel cooler when you sleep, as this will trap the breeze"*. In the intense heat, in a moment of silence and contemplation, I would envision the approach of scattered clouds, sprinkles of rain and a trailing cold wind that would ventilate the atmosphere!

Then grandma and our housemaid would try to hose off the floors by sprinkling water on the cement floor. The heat was still evident as the vapors emanated from the brick cement floor and filled the air with a refreshing aroma, a scent which I still recollect.

In order to quench our nighttime thirst, we carried terra cotta receptacles (our water coolers) which we washed, rinsed out and then filled with cold water. These were made with porous material which let a small amount of seepage through that would then evaporate and keep the water inside cold.

At nightfall, we socialized with our family and neighbors. We would have our coffee and tea with several snacks. Soon after we would all lean against the walls and watch the nightlife, entertained by the vast number of people strolling. We admired the splendor of Umma Gardens right in front of our house with its large pond, colored spotlights and fountains flowing in the immense park which faced our home close to Tahrir Square in Central Baghdad.

They used to say: "*gaze to the skies for inspiration and notice for the shooting stars, you still see them often and this will be a favorable sign. When you see that the moon is full, focus and make a wish, it will be granted!*" I am still enchanted with these beliefs because I believed in its power as the lesser light, which softened the heat of the day, now ruled the night that moved the mighty seas.

In the stillness that surrounded me, there was mystery and power in the heavens above. I felt like a descendant of the Babylonians. I believed that there was significance in the pattern of the stars and the position of the moon thereby a prophecy to foretell. I believed I was born to deliver messages through my dreams as silent knowledge surrounded me. The next morning, I had to bring my dreams into solid reality whilst I was encouraged to explain their significance.

I wondered how the Babylonians sighted the galaxy with the naked eye. Our rooftops were their observatories, and it is said that the skilled observer's visual perception was based on using polished crystal lenses to magnify the range of vision. Their ancient but advanced optical technology had magnifying properties which allowed studying the cosmos at a great distance. This 3,500-year-old piece called 'The Layard Nimrud Lens' unearthed in 1850's, is now on display at the British Museum.

They also believed the celestial realm was inhabited by gods who would protect and guide them and that their ritual moon ceremonies would bring prosperity, plentiful harvest, prevent flooding and misfortune. They were stimulated in developing a study which had lasting influence, as we still consult the daily horoscope to determine our fate.

From this place the Babylonians came to be known as the stargazers, fathers of science. They invented the zodiac wheel based on the movements of planets as well as the four phases and shapes of the moon, with the belief that they conveyed warnings and omens necessary to predict their future. The almanacs in the British Museum reveal observations by the priest astrologers, of the planetary position and the path of the moon and stars, in addition to a lunar calendar which was associated with their lives. Constellation charts were also found. They were the forefathers of our everyday practices in determining our fate by following the zodiac signs. They used logic to make their discoveries as their predictions have left a great impact on history.

The information we have acquired is recorded in the many manuscripts called 'Astronomical Diaries' which were found in the library of King Assurbanipal, inscribed on clay tablets with descriptions of their observations. The historical cuneiform texts are now in the British Museum and still have a correlation to our day to day lives. Alexander the Great ordered all these diaries to be translated into the Greek language.

At night, I always accompanied my brother (who is six years younger than me) to his bedside and I waited until he fell asleep then with a serene perspective and with a positive outlook, I set my head on my pillow said my prayers, sensed an inner peace and fell asleep.

As darkness fell, there was only a slight change in the temperature. It was time to reflect, as I held a picture in my mind, I again wished for a breath of cold air to whisk by, for a soft wind to bring some heavy clouds and force some raindrops to fall on my forehead and sway away the heat. Then I felt a delicate breeze which did not last long, but softened and ventilated the atmosphere and helped my thoughts float away. I thought to myself maybe if the sun would shrink to half its size as it rises, then we would feel half the amount of heat! Then at nighttime, the moon would soften the left-over warmth of the day.

Nighttime never scared me as I felt that the sky had thousands of eyes which watched and safeguarded me. In fact, as I collected my thoughts, I found solace as I knew that my name 'Artemis' was astrologically associated with the moon which held supremacy over the dark skies, and thus attributed to transformation, rebirth, infinity and wisdom.

Certain days I wondered what if the world suddenly remained totally dark, what if the sun stopped shedding its light? These thoughts crossed my mind as I pondered upon the salvation of mankind. Surely, we would be spared. My young mind determined that we had to be ethical with morals and not offend the eyes in the skies. Then I felt a sense of peace and my spirit was not troubled, as I drifted into deep sleep.

As dawn pronounced itself, and the silvery light of the moon dissipated, darkness gave way to a rich gold gleam of sunshine, embodied by a surge of sudden warmth. This was a wake-up call to rise and honor a new beginning. I was at a starting point again to lead a life with bliss, and I could start early on my daily duties because the hours ahead had to be productive. (I found out that successful and influential people always rise early in the morning). Moreover, I could hear the birds chirping happily while they remained invisible on the branches of the trees and I thought to myself, "*Here come the 'watchmen' of the day.*"

"There is no pillow as soft as a clear conscience".

You would ask yourself how these ancient people found their way in the dark at night. Because they were innovative, with technological advances, they invented the '**Baghdad Battery'**. With their invention, they managed to dispel the darkness and thus generate two volts of electricity and even create more light with a series of them aligned with each other.

This first source of electricity was invented in the era of 200 BC by the Parthians. The artifact was discovered in Iraq by Konig in 1800. This simple device, with its components, is housed at the National Museum of Iraq. Alessandro Volta the Italian physicist who is known to have invented the principles of electric science should have given credit to the pioneers of Mesopotamia.

BAGHDAD TOWER

This Tower is situated in the center of the city and perched at a height of 674 feet. It is the first and only revolving dining spot in Baghdad which was built as a symbol of evolution and advancement in the capital.

At a high altitude, diners would enjoy a revolving view of the city with a delightful meal whilst listening to pleasant Iraqi melodies from famous Iraqi singers. The restaurant revolved smoothly and would make a full turn every forty minutes.

Everyone enjoyed the innumerable glistening lights of the city which glowed all along the skyline and riverfront. A very enjoyable evening was spent on the revolving observation deck and in the restaurant itself as the gliding scenery increased people's interest in this city.

BAGHDAD TOWER CLOCK - For whom did this huge clock chime? Since this monument was built in the 1970s you would know that it chimed and played a tune every single hour, from a well- known anthem which paid tribute to Saddam Hussein. It resounded and was meant to be heard throughout the whole city as the voice of his ruling.

Everything here was to celebrate his life. The base was transformed into a museum. On different floors there were several exhibition halls, statues, portraits and artwork depicting his life and the major events which took place. A wide range of gifts given by foreign dignitaries were displayed everywhere. Shops, restaurants and conference halls were set up for entertainment.

Inside the hollow tower still stands a pendulum decorated with gold rifles which perpetually swings from side to side, reminding us that time is valuable and passes quickly. It leaves a shiny reflection on the marble floors of a beautiful entrance hall. This place was considered so important that its image was imprinted on the 100 Iraqi Dinar banknote.

Nowadays, at night the clock glows from afar displaying an orange background with white dials as it announces the current time. It offers a service to the people and still maintains dominance over the city since it is now an important public building as well as the Seat of the Supreme Court.

QISHLA TOWER CLOCK is a historic building which still stands proudly by the banks of the Tigris River as it towers over a panoramic sky. This landmark was built in the 1800's during the occupation of the Ottoman Turks by Sultan Abdel Hamid. The clock determined the hours of prayer and the time for the gathering of his soldiers at the barracks. The sultan felt the need to add a personal mark by encouraging advancement and progress since he valued the importance of timekeeping. Several guards were stationed on the observation tower to patrol the area and remind the inhabitants that they were always being watched for proper conduct. An inscription carved on the clock reads that it was donated by England's King George V as a gift to the Iraqi Government.

Nowadays the set of chimes is a call for you to visit the tower, as the vast landscaped green gardens and fountains render this spot very appealing. The continuous renovations of the vast interior courtyards and chambers attract many visitors, whilst a stroll on the balcony gives a grand view of the city. You will be able to visit the imperial chamber where King Faisal I was crowned. A lot of history lies within its walls.

Harun El Rashid, the caliph of Baghdad was fascinated by clocks. He thereby found a way to impress visiting dignitaries, because it was a technological advancement and keeping track of time was vital. When an alliance was to be formed between his representatives and Charlemagne's European Delegation, he decided to give Charlemagne the famous water clock, which really impressed him. This was a constructive way to bring the Christian and Islamic frontiers together in order to avoid future conflict and hostility.

I value the concept of time and as I can never turn back the clock, I consider it as a precious resource, a gift to take advantage of. At the end of the day, I ask myself what I have accomplished within the last 24 hours. It is said that: "*one thing you cannot recycle is wasted time.*"

It is important to note that Baghdad got a lot of recognition and returned to its former glory as it got nominated as the "**Capital of Arab Culture**" by the Arab League and UNESCO in 2013. Arab Senior Officials and many Heads of States from worldwide nations attended this successful event. The three-day celebration was held under huge tents and pavilions with stages, and several exhibition areas which featured art, music, folk dancing, poetry, literature, photography and theater.

Several Iraqi authors displayed their books and film producers and directors showed various clips of upcoming Iraqi films and documentaries.

Many historical sites such as the Qishla Clock, Iraqi Museums and the City of Ancient Babylon were visited whilst concerts by the Iraqi National Symphony and Ballet were performed.

Modern Fashion Shows were held in various auditoriums spread out in the capital city. A true accomplishment for Iraq.

"Embrace the beauty that your country has to offer".

MUTANABBI STREET المتنبي

There is a famous quote: "CAIRO WRITES, BEIRUT PRINTS AND BAGHDAD READS"

Throngs of people thirst for knowledge and wisdom when they visit the 'street of recovery'. Mutanabbi Street has become deservedly well known as a new era has granted the Iraqis the desire to continue their knowledge about the world.

All the stores and street vendors have their books spread on tables and shelves as well as on covered sidewalks. People are absorbed with wisdom and eagerness to educate themselves while forgetting their daily struggles.

Nowadays freedom of publishing has created a thriving business and a development to suit their interests. The second picture shows stairs from the Tigris River leading to Mutanabbi Street.

This street is named after Tayibb Al Mutanabbi, the famous classical poet who lived in the 9th century. His poetry continues to inspire the Arab world. He was born in Iraq and wrote more than three hundred and twenty poems most of which represented his own life. His popularity and courage as well as his pride and controversial personality classified him a 'wandering poet'. He lived in many Middle Eastern countries and was appointed as court poet in Syria. He did not find solace and comfort in any other country until he returned to Iraq. He believed that *"there was no wealth like knowledge, no poverty like ignorance."*

His verses speak about his philosophy in life and the narratives of many battles which are still significant and relevant nowadays. His work is still found to be fascinating and appealing and as an honor to him, a statue has been erected at the end of the street.

The statue shows the poet with his right hand raised and his left hand resting above his waist as if reciting his poem and beckoning people to rediscover his creative works. On his left is a calligraphy tool and the shaft of a feather as well as an open page with verses written on stone.

Abu Nawass Street leads to the Tigris River on the banks of which are riverfront restaurants. It is a pleasant site where one can enjoy a meal while watching the river flow. One can take a pleasant dinner cruise on the boats, enjoy a ride from the terminal or stroll through the green parks that surround the area.

SHAHBANDAR CAFÉ - The in-café' library where great minds congregate to keep the spirit of learning alive.

This is where, I was told by my grandfather, one had to be keen on learning about the history of yesterday and events of today. Situated around the corner of Mutannabi Street still stands a historical spot called 'Shahbander Café'. This is where intellectuals, writers, poets, artists, politicians and even musicians still assemble to debate on daily matters and events. It opened in 1917 and has since been very popular as people grab a seat on the wooden padded benches and discuss the topics of life.

It is a literary center where a number of people are fully involved in reading daily newspapers or devotedly absorbed in their books. The clients are mostly men and here they are storytellers who make sure memories of time are not forgotten. Layers of intellect have remained instilled in their minds which they are eager to share with others. Nowadays women find this café' of great interest too.

As soon as you sit down, you notice a relaxed atmosphere and are greeted by the patrons who are keen in acquiring knowledge. You get swept into the ongoing stories about the people in the collection of framed black and white portraits and sceneries of ancient Baghdad hanging on the walls. These resurrect the past with historical events from the kingdom of Iraq to the present day.

The favorite ritualistic beverage here is dark brewed tea served in 'estikans" (small glass teacups) - its bitter taste seems to have a connection to the difficult times during the war and the bombing of this spot in 2007. But Iraqis are brave people who believe that there are no obstacles in life which you cannot overcome. The owners offer you this robust, dark amber, highly aromatic concentrated brew which leaves a long-lasting aftertaste and advise you to enjoy your time here, sip slowly as the patrons leisurely chat and exchange ideas. Iraqis actually believe the tea's benefits as it keeps them alert and improves their concentration, eliminates toxins and lowers their stress level. They are always ready for a 'tea debate'.

The atmosphere is always bustling as some roll the 'worry beads' in their hands or play dominoes or backgammon. One notices the shelves carrying the characteristic 'dust of time' on which stand the tarnished tea pots, samovars and water jars which relate to the glorious past.

The patrons are all gathered to speak freely, as there are no restrictions or time limitations here and they interact while they express their personal views on local news and politics. Even if differences in opinion occur, it is considered very productive to make time and to share your thoughts and connect with intellectuals who are overflowing with informative knowledge in literary life. There is a sense of community in an atmosphere which is inviting because you never know which important person you might meet. *"The fate of empires depends on the education of its youth"* Aristotle

The proprietors are not focused on productivity, nor do they give importance to décor. Currently this place does not provide modern amenities, so very few patrons with electronic devices meet here as the crowd encourages conversation and exchange of thoughts. You will feel disconnected if you focus only on your laptop or phone and the regulars will regard you as 'unusual'. The primary aim is to escape from the world you are living in and enhance your knowledge about the day-to-day life.

Amidst the sounds of the clinking of tiny tea spoons, the hum of the ceiling fans as it dissipates the smoke in the air and the deep rooted aroma, the voices of knowledge loom in the atmosphere followed by pockets of laughter, and you feel inspired to believe that knowledge is power, and this will motivate you to visit 'Shahbandar Café' as its fame continues.

An Iraqi can always find the time to tell a joke. It is part of the custom as it eases the daily struggles and stress. When out and about, even riding with taxi drivers, you were always told a joke or two.

It was a competition when we gathered as to who would cause more laugher. We saw it as a coping mechanism that had a profound positive physical effect on us. I still believe that it imparts power to release tension and gives us the possibility to overcome difficulties.

So, I learned to continue with this approach to keep myself balanced. I have found it more effective to concentrate on pleasant thoughts and erase the negative ones. What is life without humor? And do you think as to how much you will help yourself psychologically? You will manage to soothe the rough edges of the days as you laugh because I truly believe there is a solution to everything.

> *"Nothing erases unpleasant thoughts more effectively than concentration on pleasant ones" Hans Selye.*

MANNA – The Noblest of all Desserts

The Tamarisk tree grows in this part of the world and yields a delicious substance called 'Manna'.

'Man El Semma', which means 'From the Heavens', is a food which appears with the morning dew on the leaves of the trees. Solid droplets amass and create a neutral, delicate odorless substance while the thin flakes are carried away by the breeze and gradually fall like frost on the ground.

It is harvested in May and the secretion which surfaces from the plant early in the morning is green in color. It has to be gathered whilst it is slightly compressed and before the sun rises, as Manna softens and dissolves rapidly.

The Tamarisk tree is tenacious and survives the hot weather. It grows in the northern part of Iraq. Manna is sold in its original state on the actual leaves cut down from branches.

Soft and hard qualities are commercialized but both are nutritive and taste equally as scrumptious.

I always remember that it was a treat to be accompanied by my grandparents Azniv and Donik to the store down the main road in Bab El Shargi, which happened to have a vast variety of Manna displayed in glass counters. I would pick various flavors and savor each bite.

It is important for me to describe the marvel that Manna can have upon you, since it is a celestial gift. Anytime, anywhere receiving a box of Manna is always appreciated and remember when you are to taste this delicacy make a wish, because it is considered as 'the bread of Heaven'.

Then the Lord said to Moses: "I am going to rain down food from heaven for you. Each day the people can go out and pick up as much food as they need for that day. I will test them in this to see whether they will follow my instructions. On the sixth day they will gather food, and when they prepare it, there will be twice as much as usual. In the evening you will have meat to eat, and in the morning, you will have <u>the bread you want</u>, then you will know that I am the Lord your God."

That evening in the desert vast numbers of quail flew in and covered the camp. The next morning the area around the camp was wet with dew, '<u>when the dew evaporated, a flaky substance as fine as frost blanketed the ground.</u>'

"This is the heavenly food the Lord has given you to eat." Moses

ABRAHAM'S WELL- EYN EL ASAD
- A force of the desert

In the province of Anbar, about 95 miles west of Baghdad, there emerges a lush green 'mirage' oasis. It seems impossible to imagine and locate a body of water amid this barren land. This is where the Prophet Abraham stopped to rest, drink and provide water for his household and followers.

On his journey in the excessive heat of the day, Abraham was grateful to come across this body of water. So he sanctified the well, as this was water for his household, herdsmen, livestock and servants while they set up their tents to rest for a few days.

He was a virtuous man, a prophet, the apostle and patriarch of his people. In a vivid vision he heard the words of God giving him the book of wisdom. So he ventured to keep his commandments through the trials of daily life. He found grace in God's eyes and was thereby blessed. His role was to make believers out of misguided pagans who honored false deities and worshipped idols. With his wise words, he managed to reach his goal. His scrolls were scriptures of the revelations he had received thereby every piece of land where he stopped and lived became a blessed spot.

The palm trees, reeds, wildflowers and waterfowl make this site a welcoming place for all. The trees were planted in a way to provide layers of shade with their beautiful fan shaped fronds making it a comfortable spot for people to rest under.

This area is called 'Eyn Al Asad' which means the 'Eye of the Lion'. Presumably lions and other wild animals roamed here. Asad palm tree groves were once abandoned but now they are being cultivated as they provide more than thirty varieties of delicious dates.

This place has been of significant importance. It is a popular belief that you can bathe here and find solace as you listen to the sounds of silence while you heal.

"Happiness should be like an oasis-the greener for the desert that surrounds it" – Rachel Field

PHOENIX DATTILIFERA - *"Someone is sitting in the shade today because someone planted a tree a long time ago" Les Brown*

Neither the strong winds, piercing sands nor intense heat can destroy the vigor and longevity of the palm tree. it grows high and mighty as the symbol of the nation.

The Babylonians believed that the palm tree evoked powerful energy representing the necessity to withstand the battles of life. They studied its development and noticed that other trees were very hard to grow whilst the Phoenix Dattilifera grew sturdy with its grounded thick roots reaching out naturally for resources from the soil.

The large fronds were a symbol of triumph and victory and were waved to welcome leaders of the nation. Also, one week before the resurrection of Christ, it is a tradition to celebrate Palm Sunday. People buy palm fronds at the church and palm crucifixes in memory of Jesus' triumphal entry into Jerusalem.

Nowadays, hundreds of qualities of dates are the second most important commodity of this land. Once a year we would travel to the lush palm groves to savor this delicious fruit. Since prehistoric days, dates have been treasured, grown to flourish and exported all over the world. They are unique and their nutritious value continue to render them necessary in our lives.

The local farmers accompanied us into the heart of an oasis as they showed us their harvesting techniques. They would point out how the palm tree thrives when the fronds are pruned at the right time as it speeds up the growth rate in clusters with many stems. They also mentioned the methods and difficult process of pollination, the transplanting of shoots to speed up growth and the tradition of weaving and braiding the leaves to create brooms, fans and baskets, and thatched rooftops.

We would watch the farmer climb the date palm retaining the ancient practice of attaching a long cord and strapping it around his waist and fastening it with a basket around the trunk of the tree. He would jump in loops with his bare feet on the tree and reach the top effortlessly. We were in awe at his agile moves to the higher levels without the use of the ladder or forklift.

Every time you eat and enjoy the flavor of dates, appreciate the efforts of the farmers.

In the city, the panorama of streets lined with the trees adds beauty, exotic scenery and character whilst providing a graceful shade and a welcome relief from the heat.

Incidentally, the Christmas tree will be prevalent everywhere in Baghdad as the Iraqi Federal Government in 1918 declared Christmas to be a National Holiday to celebrate the birth of Christ for which we express our appreciation and gratitude.

"In all things of nature, there is something of the marvelous" Aristotle

FLYING CARPETS

Yes we believe in flying carpets, especially after reading the fables of 1,001 Nights.

I remember when autumn arrived, we would fetch our carpets which were stored away in the cellars. Our house cleaners unrolled them on our patios to air-out the strong odor of crushed mothballs. They were then cleaned and placed elegantly on the floors to transform and embellish the rooms. I remember the "Kashan" and "Bukhara" valued Persian brands and yearly we would purchase others to bestow beauty to our home.

There was a sense of delight as we admired the vivid patterns and rich colors. They were adorned with elaborate motifs of flowers, trees, plants as well as mythical animals and intricate geometric figures which resembled the beauty of a spring garden. Owning carpets was a matter of status and one's wealth was measured by its antiquity. The older the carpet, the more valuable it became.

In downtown Baghdad, on Rashid Street, all the vendors placed the carpets on the sidewalks and allowed pedestrians to walk over them. This was done so the wear and tear would enrich and embolden the colors.

Later it became fashionable to buy smaller silk rugs and adorn the walls. The homes became an exhibition spot as we preserved the handmade commodities. Iraqi and Armenian carpets later began being marketed and soon became very popular and more affordable. The carpet weaving industries in Northern Iraq practiced an ancient craft which allowed artisans to learn this valuable and very profitable trade.

The carpet in our hallway was chosen as the 'magic carpet'. I remember my grandparents telling me that after I went to sleep, it would fly up to the sky and then would land back in our house before we awoke.

I continued to believe the story, when in the mornings, I would notice that the carpet had shifted from its one side of the hall to the other. Then I was told to turn the corners of the carpet, as there would be a surprise. My grandparents would disappear into the other rooms and would say that Aladdin's genie had brought me some Iraqi dinars for good luck. Imagine the look on my face as I surprisingly picked the money up with joy. I told myself *"I would never be selfish, and Grandma and Grandpa would love some magical Manna treats. This I will spend on them"*.

When winter was over and spring came along, we once again spread the crushed mothballs all around the rugs and wrapped them with a plastic cover to store away and lie dormant during the upcoming hot days.

"Value your carpet and it will never let you down"!

CTESIPHON – A residence to match the King's prestige

As you drive south of Baghdad, you will reach the city of Salman Pak and you will discover an imposing monument in Ctesiphon, which was once a structure built to delight spectators.

This was the Imperial palace of King Khosrau, his 'Winter Palace', where he chose to live while Ctesiphon became one of the most important cities in the world. The massive arch in the photo is 84 feet wide and 120 feet high. Only the left-wing façade remains. One can only imagine the immensity of the maze of audience rooms, chambers, hallways, and galleries. It is also known to be the largest single brick span vault in the whole world.

This remaining facade now standing is still regarded as an admirable masterpiece of ancient architecture. One's imagination can run wild thinking about its opulence during the king's reign.

The ever-flowing Tigris River nearby made this spot salubrious for Khosrau. The victorious king did not want to be forgotten in time, nor be part of a lost city, so he commissioned the building of the biggest single span built of mud bricks.

The Sassanid leader reigned successfully. He was crowned in this city and was named 'the king of good fortunes'. He gradually developed the land and received his guests with the aim of developing a trade of carpet weaving.

His intention was to impress visiting dignitaries and notables, so he offered further interest to them by adding beauty and opulence to his throne room. To show that he lived in regal style, this was to be his propaganda. He commissioned hundreds of artisans to weave the 'eternal' carpet to cover the main banquet floor. The woven silk carpet was to resemble a massive paradisiac garden. It is said that the oriental motifs had flora and fauna designs elegantly styled with patterns of bold colored trees in addition to medallions encircled with images of birds encrusted with pearls and jewels. He believed it was welcoming for his guest and added warmth and elegance to the environment.

Elaborate tapestries made of gold cloth graced the walls as the vibrancy of its colors glistened. The luxurious imperial chambers lead to inner open courtyards while processional galleries opened into landscaped gardens embellished with splashing fountains. This was all designed to impress visitors as they paid tribute to the king while they were welcomed with lavishness and generosity. The King's astuteness and wisdom attracted merchants and tradesmen thereby the city evolved into a rich center where an industry prospered. He became known as 'Bearer of Good Fortunes'.

He fell in love and married Shirin, an Armenian Princess whom he esteemed. He granted her his entire wealth and kingdom. She was well known for her intellect and recognized for her aptitude in day-to-day matters. His affection for his beloved wife awoke the interest of many poets including Ganjavi Alzami, who referred to it as the *"sweetest love story in the world and by truth there is no sweeter than it".*

Ctesiphon's splendor ceased when the Mongols destroyed and ransacked the area and it slipped into complete neglect under their rule. The Mongols consequently never managed to prosper or succeed, but only failed and deteriorated. They could not wipe out historical facts and whatever remains we still value. *"Remember that all through history, there have been tyrants and murderers and evil doers. For a time, they seem invincible. But in the end, they always fall. ALWAYS. "* Mahatma Gandhi

During springtime, we often planned picnic excursions to Ctesiphon. On weekends, we needed a break from the busy capital city. We would prepare the baskets and iceboxes together with folding chairs and tables. We looked forward to our outdoor meals in an open-air environment. We would gather with family, friends, and neighbors, whilst we listened to music from the portable radios and the record player mounted in the car.

For me it was a memorable outdoor reception on royal grounds, since I was familiar with the history behind this monumental palace. I would listen to the tales told by the local people which made the hours more intriguing.

The family event started with refreshing salads, hors d'oeuvres and a vast array of hearty sandwiches. There would be plates of pickles, cheese and olives, all artfully spread on the tables. On some occasions, we used our portable charcoal grills and barbecued kebabs with lots of vegetables, while we cut the watermelons and cantaloupes in large slices and set them on ice slabs.

At the end of the meal on kebab days, I watched the coal embers glow in red and yellow colors. It was then time to place the coffee jugs on the heat and wait for the water to boil in order to prepare Armenian coffee. Tea was also made in samovars. The baklavas and cakes then were cut and served. It was a day of food and pleasure, and I enjoyed the afternoon, while recapturing further clues to the past surrounding this sumptuous palace.

Welcome To Iraq"

مرحبا بكم في العراق

ISHTAR, THE CEREMONIAL ENTRY GATE

At the entrance of the city of Babylon is the Ishtar Gate dedicated to Ishtar, goddess of fertility, war and love. It was built by King Nabuchadnezzar in 575 B.C. It is an outstanding entryway made of cedar wood, and adorned with decorative motifs of lions, bulls, dragons and aurochs. They were covered with beautiful blue enameled glazed tiles, in lapis lazuli, to give a glossy vibrant colorful shine from afar to make visitors gaze at its wonder.

The ceremonial gate leads you to the Processional Way, which stretches for half a mile to the ziggurats and to the gate of Marduk. Ishtar gate was the triumphal entry point for New Year parade celebrations, which every individual had to participate in order to be bestowed with good luck and fortunes. It leads to the Processional Sacred Street which was flanked by high surrounding walls and statues and lined on each side by colonnades. It was once considered one of the marvels of the ancient world.

"History begins here".

Lion of Babylon

Do not disturb our ever-shifting sands with bad intentions because the silent voice of the desert speaks out loud to the Universe.

Behold, the lion of Babylon guards the entrance to the Processional Way in Babylon. This is a famous landmark, which was regarded as an emblem of power. The significance of an immense lion trampling over a man symbolizes that if one entered the city with ill intentions, one would be defeated.

Lions were considered sacred animals and were venerated by the inhabitants of Babylon, since in every form of art they were depicted on murals and decorated on ceramic friezes. This striding lion image was found at the entrance of the king's throne room made of colored blue glazed bricks.

Although the facial features of the lion have been damaged through time, the entire body still stands.

The statue which is situated on a large pedestal, was carved on basalt rock, with the intent to withstand the torrid heat and sandstorms.

As evidenced by history, and still prevalent, the events of the past serve as a good lesson for those who have the intention to invade Iraq for they shall never prevail. They come and go just like the ripples of a fast-flowing river downstream.

*"The past is a source of knowledge and the future is
a source of hope"* Stephen Ambrose

BABYLON – ONE OF THE SEVEN WONDERS OF THE WORLD - Civilization and knowledge still lie within its walls

The famous city of Babylon whose name is known worldwide lies in Hillah approximately 53 miles south of the capital city of Baghdad. It is visible among the ruins and still holds importance due to the mighty golden age of Hammurabi and Nebuchadnezzar, who reigned here, and whose imprints are still visible on the ancient bricks.

The traces of an advanced civilization and culture lie under the mounds. They are the remains of the past and bear witness to a rich empire. At this site, amongst the sleepy remains of an ancient empire, you may even hear slight sounds from the sands.

Babylon was a commercial and literary religious center where agriculture was developed. Following the path of the river Euphrates, this city was often partly consumed after the annual flooding as water spilled over its banks. It had a moat surrounding it so the metropolis was not swept away. It survived as remains of the ancient ruins testify to the glorious past. The river then created a fertile landscape but has since diverted its course and winds a long distance away from this city.

If you are searching for clues, you will notice that the original bricks still bear inscriptions praising King Nabuchadnezzar. Each old brick bears layers of civilization still affecting our lives. There are also high fortification walls to the right and to the left.

On the east side of the street is the reconstructed temple Nin Makh. The Southern Palace lies to the left side and has been rebuilt. New bricks have been set over the main ancient foundation. It has several courtyards with halls and chambers and a vast throne and court room. This was the King's main residence, surrounded by many public building structures and religious centers.

It is presumed that the foundation at the north-eastern corner of the Southern Palace was one of the only remnants of the Hanging Gardens of Babylon. As we slope down

from this area, we see a ziggurat enclosure and Marduk Temple, also built by Nabuchadnezzar. The Summer Palace stands on a high mound northward with substructures built below the walls containing ventilation shafts leading to the rooms and halls of the palace. It was here that Nebuchanezzar resorted to during the hot summer months. To the side of Nabuchandezzar's palace, on the hilltop, overlooking the Euphrates River lies a modern, vast and lavish palace, four stories high, shaped like a stepped pyramid. It does not seem to integrate in the historical site but still holds fascination. It is a real contrast to the environment as it was built in the 1970's and yet remains mystical and attracts curious visitors. It contains large rooms, marble staircases and floors, massive chandeliers and ornate ceilings and murals.

Reconstructed Processional Way at Pergamon Museum

At the time of its glory, Babylon celebrated the arrival of New Year. The festivals were called Akitu. Everyone participated to honor the gods, to bring their offerings and gifts

 to a beautiful setting. Floral garlands, bouquets of flowers and colorful ribbons decorated the people and decked the walls. The high priest commenced and directed the procession. As the chariots passed, the women would scatter flower petals to the wind and pray for abundance, ensuring plentiful harvest and good health. They lit fires and paid tribute to deities by chanting and dancing on their way to the main temple of Marduk, all along the Processional Way.

In the 1970s, once again, Babylon came alive, as the famous 'International Festival' was held once a year. Great performers from all over the world would share their exquisite talents which were staged in the courtyard of the southern palace and also in the new theater. The festival always drew large crowds internationally as they would conjure up a vivid picture of ancient celebrations of the past.

The program included operas, rock music, modern and symphony groups as well as ballet dancers, acrobats, traditional Iraqi singers and orchestras. The whole arena and its surroundings would be bright with colorful lights focused on the palace during the evening performance. Once again Babylon would come alive and from a distance, people could hear the echoes of the sounding music.

There also existed two museums containing authentic antiquities and relics of the past, which were displayed on glass shelves in large cases of the various halls. Babylon still lives and will be restored to its ancient glory and will again pulsate with life. It will develop into a famous tourism center once again.

It bears the burdens of time yet reveals intriguing clues to a glorious past of an optimistic civilization. Herodotus, the famous historian 485 B.C., claimed: "*Babylon is a 'grain bearing' country, and in addition to its size, it surpasses in <u>splendor</u> any city in the known world.*"

Even nowadays, the name 'Babylon' has a strong lasting appeal. Its name will last as long as time. Visit Babylon on 'You Tube – Babylon Eagle Eye'

Original Song dedicated to Babylon lyrics and music by my son Manuel

Babylon calls to us over desert sands of years gone by
Babylon beckons us like a magic carpet in the sky
Stay One Thousand One Nights by my side
As the Tigris River turns the tide
Come along, you belong, Oh Babylon!

Babylon, a mirage when you close your eyes
You are bound to see
Babylon shields my heart like the ancient leaves of the old palm tree
Hanging Gardens for a dream like you
Manna falling from the sky of blue
You belong, come along, Oh Babylon!

Babylon sail with me the Euphrates winding waterways
Babylon hold my hand under Adam's Tree with me always stay
Open up your heart like the Ishtar Gate it takes a lifetime I will wait
Come along, you belong, Oh Babylon

Papken Khatchadurian
in Baghdad 2022

113

PROCESSION STREET – BABYLON – The Street that launched civilization

Procession Street was a magnificent thoroughfare and is still in existence. It is in its natural original state, paved with ancient stones and bitumen, flanked on both sides by high restored walls. It passes through the Ishtar Gate and slopes south, then turns west leading to the Marduk Temple.

Procession Street courtesy of Linda Ohanian

One can envision the splendor of the vibrant Babylonian celebrations and festivities to welcome the New Year, which were devoted to their deity Marduk. The ceremonies were performed with parades and chariot floats. People would be draped in vivid colorful attire, bearing gifts, singing praise and chanting rhythms. They were accompanied by musicians who danced to the sound of drums.

Here was a bountiful display where decorated walls were festooned and draped with arrangements of flowers, vines and branches of palm trees. People flowed into the street to pay homage to their god, to be bestowed with good luck and abundant harvest for the upcoming New Year.

They carried icons for protection whilst they scattered petals of multicolored blossoms and garlands which carpeted the street and perfumed the air. As they hurled the flowers to the heavens, they asked for good fortune and miracles. They believed the message would be carried away by the wind into the skies to be granted long life and salvation.

People would celebrate until they reached their destination, the Etemenanki Shrine. They brought gifts and herds of animals as offerings to captivate the attention of the gods. They had to be generous to receive abundance and enlightenment in their lives.

As dusk crept in, Procession Street and its surroundings would glow with hundreds of lights flickering as more people crowded the area with handheld lanterns and torches. Along the walls people would lean from their balconies and windows lit by candles. In good spirit they sang and filled the air with their songs of praise by welcoming the ongoing parade.

Nowadays, if you were to walk on the original discolored stone pavement, you can sense the mysterious forces revive the splendor of the past.

"We cannot hold a torch to light another's path without brightening our own" Ben Sweetland

Modern Palace on Euphrates-Offers
a grand view of Babylon

Amongst the ancient ruins of the Babylonian era, perched on a man-made hill, is a structure known as the new modern Palace of Babylon. It has many large royal rooms, marble staircases and floors, massive chandeliers, ornate ceilings and frescoed walls. Saddam Hussein built this lavish palace in the 1970's with a great panoramic view of the flowing Euphrates. Unfortunately, it is now an empty palace, with graffiti all over the walls. You would wonder why it stands in solitude. Is it because it was built over resting grounds? Silent graves now desire movement and activity by visitors, in order to render it a happy place, now belonging to Iraqi people. Hopefully with the new Government projects in line, it will soon be cleaned up and restored to its original status.

<u>Visions of grandeur to last forever</u> -Nowadays the walls of Babylon still speak to us through inscriptions. The faded inscriptions still existing in cuneiform writing on bricks, date back thousands of years. Some of them mention Nabuchadnezzar as the ruling King who restored the city of Babylon back to its ancient glory. He rebuilt the crumbling city to make it the envy of its neighboring countries.

"Nabuchadnezzar King am I, of Babylon, son of Nabopolasars, who cares for temples of Esagila and Ezida has reconstructed the whole city of Babylon."

Saddam Hussein was inspired by the late King's accomplishments and thereby declared himself a descendant of King Nebuchadnezzar. He wanted his name to remain everlasting. So, he followed this example of self-importance and had bricks stamped in Arabic which are <u>still visible</u> on the new walls erected on top of the old historic foundations. He went on a large-scale rebuilding project and restored the ancient imperial grounds.

It reads: *"Built by Saddam Hussein, son of Nabuchadnezzar, descendent of old rulers, to glorify Iraq"*.

Buried in the foundations, a clay brick was also found which is now at the 'Museum of the Bible'. Written in cuneiform it describes the restoration of the whole city, the building of several palaces and the glory of the King.

While many leaders have come to power with fairness and honesty, others have elevated their importance by having an inflated sense of self.

With an arsenal of unconfronted power, their self-worth could be heightened to everlasting proportions.

<u>Where does the saying *"The Writing is on the Wall"* originate from?</u>

King Belshazzar was the grandson of Nabuchadnezzar. He believed in pagan gods and held several lavish feasts to honor them. He was an arrogant man who believed he was invincible and practiced over- indulgence. One evening during festivities, he ordered the exotic goblets of silver and gold to be filled with wine for the lords and ladies to drink as an honor to the gods. Little did he know that these were the temple treasures stolen by King Nabucadnezzar during his various sieges against Jerusalem where the population was captured and enslaved.

During their merriment, the room lightened up with a hand that spelled out a direct message on the wall. Belshazzar remained alarmed and in total shock because he could not understand the meaning.

He stood in fear and called on the enchanters, magicians, and astrologers to decipher the meaning. But they failed, and he is advised to summon Daniel, a wise spiritual slave.

Daniel read the message. He said:" *Your kingdom and empire will be overthrown very soon*". Sure enough in the following days, the Persians and the Medes defeated and conquered his sovereignty. Thus, the meaning of the saying "*It is written on the wall*" is "*a warning that everything is obviously scripted before you. Heed to it*".

The reception hall is vast and spacious with marble floors, elaborate frescoes on the ceilings and mirrored panels on the walls. The banquet rooms and state rooms, with several balconies, are meant to be guest rooms with alluring views of the river which capture the whole panorama of Babylon city.

The palace and its grounds have acquired the benevolence of the Iraqi people. It still is a place of interest to the locals and tourists who have the pleasure of visiting the gardens surrounded by rosebuds and exotic plants. They have picnics on the vast veranda facing the river and remain awed by its splendor. The palace, with its quiet reflection, remains haunted by lavish mysteries. It also has to be restored and cleaned up by the authorities who have this planned soon.

"If a test of civilization be sought, no one can be so sure as to the condition of that half of society over which the other half has power." Harriet Martineau.

BABYLON THEATER- MODERN FESTIVALS

Babylon was alive once again in 1987 with the opening of the International Festival which was held around the ancient ruins. The colorful show of innumerable lights, floodlit arches, and music resounding in the air, made the city of Babylon breathe

once again for an entire month. Under the star-studded skies, you were greeted by women dressed in long gowns waving feathery palm branches welcoming you with a smile as men draped in robes held lit torches to radiate and revive the ancient glory of the city.

Fifty countries brought their top talented performers. Concerts, ballet, folklore groups, pianists, soloists, vocalists, acrobats and operas performed together with the splendid Iraqi National Symphony. The place was packed with people from all over the world in the presence of an ancient civilization where you could enjoy a guided tour, as well as the pleasure of passing an enjoyable evening filled with live entertainment. I remember visitors saying that they were transported back in time and the ambience took them back to the days of splendor and past glories. The sounds of music echoed and resonated in the air and the colorful sights on stage brought delight as people clapped in joy. Once this festival is re-launched by the Tourism Ministry, it will once again attract people from all over the globe.

"Study the past, if you would divine the future" Confucius

BABEL TOWER

In the kingdom of Babel, King Nimrod was born. He became known as the 'warrior', fierce and cruel to his people.

In his aspiration to become the most famous ruler, he had a great tower built to reach the sky in order to discover the mystery of the heavens. He was an inquisitive and curious man and believed that nothing was impossible. He wanted to be able to communicate with God and his wishes were to 'keep his people united 'and 'to spare him from death'.

"Let us reach glory and fame in the world and discover what is beyond the unknown" was his motto and his motive to build this tower.

He was mistaken in his approach for as soon as the shrine was assembled, unethical acts such as human and animal sacrifices took place.

The temple was built as a stairway but could not survive with only mud and straw formed into sunbaked bricks plastered with bitumen.

So in the land of Shinar he proceeded with his mission to build a stronger structure but the number of laborers was not sufficient. People of different races, skilled artisans and craftsmen, master builders and planners were brought in from neighboring countries so as to accelerate the construction.

As the number of people increased, so did trouble. Matters got more complicated and misunderstood. This impeded and interfered with the progress. Hence there was confusion, misinterpretation of languages and operations. The people soon could no longer communicate and understand each other. Thereby the well-known phrase *"the confusion of languages"*.

The tower was ill fated and remained unfinished as Nimrod's ultimate wish was not accomplished. As time went by, the building subsequently crumbled and was burned down. And soon after, the whole city was plundered and destroyed together with all its buildings.

Only the foundation was found, as mentioned by Pietro Della Valle in his expedition in 1650. It is assumed that the tower was circular with ascending stairs with a series of terraced floors broader on lower levels and sequentially narrower on higher levels. A shrine and watchtower were on the upper higher level dedicated to their god Bel.

"Always do what is right in God's eyes" because an ancient Chinese proverb says "when you do wrong then you and your children will bear the consequence".

GREEK AMPHITHEATER- BABEL -SELEUCID ERA IN MESOPOTAMIA

Alexander the Great of Macedonia conquered Babylon, and decided to set up his capital here during the Seleucid Empire. The Hellenistic town was founded by the Tigris River. Alexander had this amphitheater built to honor Dionysus, the god of wine, to honor his own victory, and to entertain and show appreciation to his army and higher officials. Babylon was a place that fascinated him. He noticed a highly developed society where there was evidence of progress and people lived harmoniously. He decided to establish his final residence here.

An alliance was made with the Babylonians, Chaldeans and Persians. Their political, military and administrative habits appealed to him. Also, the culture and loyal kinship of these people made a positive significant impact on Alexander.

There in the 'land of plenty' was evidence of progress and agricultural wealth within the Fertile Crescent. A wide expanse of land could be further developed by a system of irrigation from the river Euphrates, the lifeline for cultivation, and the river flotilla would commence trade with neighboring countries. He could stabilize the nation, regulate trade, unify the monetary system and introduce democracy in addition to Greek culture.

Alexander stressed that the use of the land was not to go to waste. He developed a passion in growing wheat which would feed all the people in this region. His clear vision of the warm sun, the rich miracle of silt and lush soil would yield fine healthy crops. He found great satisfaction and passion in observing the seedlings grow. He had a particular focus on reaping a bountiful harvest with the help of landowners who earned the most profitable income.

In a way he envisioned that this was an example to follow in everyday life which would also make good use of nature's gifts. These elements meant that even people could transition to a new existence, with a new enriched soul, to resume life and to advance.

He wanted to gain more prestige by forming a coalition while encouraging mixed marriages between the Macedonian men and local women of this land so as to create mixed noble blood amongst his officers.

He allied all the forces and wanted to unite the East with the West. He created support and security to maintain a satisfied army who would not get dispirited or feel homesick. He thought of ways to gratify the people and win their favor. He believed that it was important to preserve and incorporate the cultures and customs and to assimilate into a Hellenic world.

But most importantly there had to be time for celebrations and festivities. He ventured on building an amphitheater to create festivals with music and dancing, food, and wine. He would introduce western theater and the arts.

The semi- circular structure was built similar to the famed site in Delphi Greece. Since there were no sloping verdant hills, Alexander decided to embellish the place with lush vegetation.

Alexander was a spiritual individual. Once he was a warrior, but now a seeker of peace. He became a mystical leader who was intrigued to discover that the Babylonians were the first civilization to study the rise and setting of planets. Their calculations based on the position of the stars and motion of the moon.

Here the sky-watchers determined the fate of mankind as the celestial realm held the secret to their destiny. This captivated Alexander's interest so he immediately embraced and followed the teachings as he introduced Babylonian astronomy to Greek society. He felt there was definitely a correlation between astronomy and Greek astrology, so he brought the study back to Greece.

Alexander continued to be a firm believer in the supernatural forces and oracular mystical powers which played an active role in his life. Several times during the year, when he felt troubled by the strain in his life or sensed his powers of resistance weakening, he set off on his mission to Greece to consult the prophecies of the priestess in order to regain encouragement. He went to purify himself, to strengthen his soul and overcome negativity with the healing properties of the Castilian fountains. With votive offerings, he approached the priestess of Delphi and asked for protective spells.

He would carry the beneficence he acquired back to Babylon as he believed he would become divine in the presence of the Greek priestess sitting on her stool. She would close her eyes, meditate and inhale the hallucinogenic mystique vapors floating out of underground hot streams. She would then chant and fall into a trance and murmur words as well as ominous warnings for favorable and unfavorable times. Alexander made sure to document the delivered oracles because they were associated and inspired by Apollo.

He was tired of battles and bloodshed, so it was time to re-kindle his soul. He was seeking peace and wisdom to free him from mental strain, fear and anger in n addition to sustain and find common ground with the people while ruling and organizing his new empire.

He learned the art of meditation by seeking inner harmony, shifting tension to bring clarity and tolerance with inner silence. His theory must have been to "*listen to the sounds of silence*". He thus surrendered to a new life feeling revitalized with spiritual evolvement. This was also a tool for self-understanding and a way to discipline the mind. He lived in a world of uncertainty and at times he did not pay heed to unfavorable circumstances.

Under the nearby mounds at Tel Umar, archaeologists found masks and statues of Dionysus. It is believed that Alexander worshipped this god whose mask had vines and grapes interlaced on a crown holding a magic wand and a cup of wine. He alleged that the fruit of the vine appeased problems, alleviated daily impediments because jovial disposition resolved his tribulations.

The arena was set up in a perfect position; right on the riverfront where the life-giving waters ran swift and carried the bounty of rich deposits to irrigate the fertile soil. The valley of sunshine was blissful as this is where his people would attain deep gratification by harvesting the waters of the winter skies and feed it to lavish land, a method of taming the desert.

When Alexander returned from Greece, festivals were held for the patron god of theater Dionysus . Banquets, lavish musical entertainment and public games were added to the feast. Also, he introduced Greek plays, tragedies and comedies which were performed by several male actors, narrators and commentators.

Most probably he set up a quiet tranquil retreat for rest and contemplation. Vast water gardens surrounded with a multitude of trees, vineyards interlaced on ornate trellises created shady lanes and paths along raised platforms with pavilions.

Although this theater still stands the test of time, in the wilderness near Babel, close to Babylon, one can still capture the vision of lush sprawling green vistas, galleries and courtyards. It had terraces sprouting with shrubs, plains and meadows with warm scented flowers to add fragrance in the air, set up by the river canals with overlapping foliage grown to wrap around graceful columns with rose petals scattered on the decks. Just as they honored springtime, I honored it too. In my little world, I showed gratitude towards nature and genuinely delighted in watching the fruit and vegetables that I had planted sprout in our garden. I found great pleasure in discovering daily the blossoming of flowers and examining the new stems bearing melons, watermelons, zucchini, and cucumbers. They lay completely covered and concealed under the large overlapping leaves that had captured the sunlight, as if to say *"I remain hidden mysteriously now in the shade, you will see me, when I am ripe."* Was it the river water with its rich nutrients that rendered the fertility of the soil? The radiance of the sun that ripened and rendered the sweetest flavorsome nourishment on my table? It satisfied not only me but also whoever shared my food. I thought that I could associate the above to our lives and thereby sow seeds of wisdom so as to cultivate kindness, compassion and understanding. *"As she has planted, so does she harvest, such is the field of Karma"* Sri Guru Granth Sahib. Alexander also felt that this land could not lose its vitality and that music and dancing had healing properties. Thus, you have to believe that the aspect of entertainment always gives pleasure and delight. It has a beneficial positive effect by leading people to have a happy outlook on life.

Alexander travelled to Nineveh to discover the famous royal library of King Ashurbanipal of Assyria. He was inspired by the texts chronicled by a literate congregation. This center of learning contained thousands of tablets written by scholars, teachers, philosophers and scientists. This motivated him to continue to keep the spirit of learning alive. His aim was to educate Greek society about the advanced culture of this nation and to set up a library in Babel. High-level minds would work together to translate, propagate and enlighten knowledge of a new world. He envisioned the creation of 'an oasis of wisdom', which would incorporate Neo-Assyrian teachings to Hellenistic ones. He envisioned the destiny of his empire to be dependent on culture advancement. Unfortunately, Alexander died young but left his legacy to Ptolemy, the Greek General who was his associate, his friend, and successor.

Nowadays when you visit Mutannabi Street where hundreds of book vendors are present, you will see an enthusiastic crowd gather with keenness for knowledge. This street leads to 'Cafe' Shahbander' where you will see intellectuals congregate to teach about the great history of our nation, by conversing and educating the patrons. So you can see that the quest for knowledge thereby continues.

"Lives of great men all remind us we can make our lives sublime. And, departing, leave behind us footprints on the sands of time" –Henry Wadsworth Longfellow

NABUCHADNEZZAR AND THE HANGING GARDENS OF BABYLON- A highly developed society!
One of the Seven Wonders of the World.

THE HANGING GARDENS OF ANCIENT BABYLON.

The Hanging Gardens of Babylon had several terraced flat roofs with trees and plants which would overhang on the walls and were fed by chain pulley pumps. They would withdraw the water from the Euphrates River, raise it and empty it into a well with ducts while diverting the water to soak the plants. Here was the 'Fertile Crescent'.

How far would you go in life to please your wife? The answer lies in King Nebuchadnezzar's life.

He believed that there was an underlying message in each reverie. He tried to understand the meaning and discover what significance it would have.

He was a Babylonian king (605-562 B.C.) who was fascinated in exploring all his dreams.

He was so mystified and curious that for each dream he would try to gain insight and understanding by consulting wise men, astrologists, magicians and sorcerers.

Nabuchadnezzar thought that his life had to be foretold and thereby he would be saved from disasters, conquests, difficulties and death. Sure enough, the prophecies which were predicted helped him become a powerful ruler.

King Nabuchadnezzar II

This king was of Chaldean origin and reigned for more than forty years while achieving vast military conquests. He restored Babylon and rebuilt the whole city.

One night he dreamed of a nearby powerful tribe overthrowing his kingdom. This was a message for him to put an end to fighting and become diplomatically involved with the neighboring countries.

It was also time to settle down with a wife. He decided to take a short trip to the Median green hilltops where he met and fell in love with Amytis from Medes. He found her to be beautiful, intelligent, well poised and graceful and immediately decided to marry her. This would also aid in creating an alliance with her nation.

Time went by and the king was content with all his achievements. He was glorified and felt he was invincible and that nothing could stop him. He wanted to be worshipped so he erected a gold idol in his image in front of one of the Babylonian gates.

Amytis was happy in the beginning but, after a year, she began showing discontentment and unhappiness. She was surrounded by barren grounds and wanted to leave. She longed for her hometown of lush fertile land of green hills and meadows, rich vegetation, and cool weather. She was tired of the desert, which depressed and disheartened her.

The queen was strong and decided to confront Nabuchadnezzar with her feelings and intentions. The king listened with great interest but was soon shocked and thought wholeheartedly that he had acted selfishly and had not paid attention to her wellbeing.

He truly loved her and felt he could not live without her, nor could he let her venture away. He thought to himself: *"I have restored Babylon with my might, I have changed my ways to satisfy my people, I have made this land prosperous but now it is time to concentrate on my beloved wife. How could I live without my queen? I will bring the mountains to her and I will build the mightiest palace worthy of her beauty, thus I will satisfy her."*

So a major undertaking took place. It would be a site for two impressive palaces with tiers of sloped vaulted terraces, mimicking mountains, raised one above the other, filled with earth, planted with flowers, trees, bushes and plants brought in from all over the world. They were to be richly adorned with sculptures and vases flowing with vegetation and greenery of all sorts. Colorful flora was added to inspire and bring the queen happiness, trees from various nations and blossoming shrubs were planted to sweeten the air around her.

Reaching far up to the skies the palace was erected close to the Euphrates, to provide an irrigation system with underground canals. It would be fed by the river and which would be raised with chain pumps attached to buckets to tip and dump over the plants, refreshing them to remain evergreen. The best planners, engineers, laborers, masons and brick layers were brought to the land for this important mission which eventually delighted any spectator. The king said: *"Is this not the great Babylon that I have built for a royal residence by my mighty strength and for my majestic honor?"* Daniel 4:30

The Hanging Gardens of Babylon, one of the Seven Wonders of the World. Here was a magnificent and elaborate undertaking which did please Amytis. Nabuchadnezzar's intense love for her was confirmed, as he had gone to great lengths to make her feel that this was her new home. Amytis was now content and satisfied because the king had sought to bring her happiness.

She convinced herself that King Nabuchadnezzar was truly the man of her life; thereby she remained dedicated and devoted until the end.

'Strabo', the famous geographer and historian, and 'Philo of Byzantine' in their ancient writings, mention Babylon's Hanging Gardens in their writings.

The famous clay cylinder of Nabuchadnezzar reveals the existence of his lush, sophisticated palaces. A cylinder was intentionally interred under the foundation of the buildings so as to reveal to the world their heritage and power. It was carved in cuneiform script and is currently exhibited at the British Museum, Room 55.

NEBUCHADNEZZAR ON HIS THRONE.

You can identify Nabuchadnezzar's name inscribed on certain bricks still existing on the original foundations, as he did not desire his memory to vanish throughout history. This was meant to remind people that his fame would not end and he would remain the king for eternity.

Impressed by this story, Giuseppe Verdi composed an Italian opera called "_Nabucco_" in which he states: "*This is the opera with which my artistic career really begins and though I had many difficulties to fight about it, it is certain that '_Nabucco_' was born under a lucky star.*"

"There is no substitute for the comfort supplied by the utterly taken for granted relationship."

Iris Murdoch

Southern Iraq Home of unique bird 'reed warbler' - untouched by the modern world

As we travel south and reach Nassiriyah, the landscape changes and you find yourself amidst the wetlands of Iraq.

The Marsh Arabs have dwelled in these wetlands for centuries, since Sumerian times, and not much has changed in their daily lives. It seems that the world has come to a standstill here.

The floating reed huts are habitats which all belong to one hundred thirty families. They live on the man-made floating islands in huts made of reed, mud, bitumen and clay and anchored to palm trees. They are built without the use of nails, screws, cement or wood. Large quantities of tall reeds and tall grass are bunched together to create the pillars and the skeleton frame to which they add the reed mats.

The lush long-stemmed reeds, shrubs and grass abound here as well as the water fowl, water buffalo and various wildlife. In the 1990's this whole area was drained because of a conflict with the government and the lack of water forced many people to leave.

Now these territories have been replenished and breathe once again as people gradually return to their wetlands with optimism of a better life. Their livelihood depends on raising livestock, herding water buffalo, hunting, fishing, and weaving baskets, mats and hand-made carpets.

Hospitality reigns in these wetlands and to my best knowledge these are the only people who build a second, better quality hut next to their modest ones to welcome their guests and offer them comfort. The previous photo shows the interior of these Mudhiffs where the sheiks meet their visitors.

The canals are the thoroughfares. The only way to travel is in slender long boats called 'mashoof' which glide all around the intricate network of waterways, winding through tall thickets of shrubs.

With the recovery of the region, it is so nice to welcome the 'Reed Warbler' chirping rhythmically and happily as if singing a love song. The' least known bird' in the world finds solace here and results as the indicator of rebirth in the region. Easily heard but rarely seen, this 'Old World Eurasian Songbird' breeds only on these shallow waters and anticipates a yearning for a new life. It is an interesting creature who hides away amongst the tall reeds as it builds its cup shaped nest and diligently protects its territory.

The locals say that while this bird sings it conveys a message that life is returning to normal and that it does not want to be just a visitor but a resident. It wants to establish its territory permanently and protect the marshes by being an avid insect catcher during its low flights across the waterways. The sunset and sunrise chorus of high-pitched chirps are the wake-up call of their survival.

It is to express that the eco-system is healing while other migratory birds such as ducks, flamingos and pelicans join them. Bird watchers have classified them as a very intelligent species, not too friendly, yet alert while to warn others if danger is around.

Every day the Marsh dwellers strive to improve and better their lives in a harsh environment. New educational programs to avoid pollution are being set up, as well as electricity, clean running water stations, better sanitation and heating systems for the cold season. The Ma'dan believe that the good life will bounce back as peace drifts by the re-flooding of the wetlands which is also their main source of drinking water.

All the men wear long robes (dishdashas) with turbans (Igals) twisted around their heads whilst the women wear their abayas. Although they just seem to float around, they are content to remain oblivious about life elsewhere.

As soon as a visitor arrives, one tribesman blows a horn to convey the approach of visitants arriving at their territory. They communicate from afar as to who the newcomers are and thereafter, they safely glide to the shore in their boats to greet them.

If you ever encounter a wedding here, you will be immediately invited to join as weddings are events of a lifetime. After the official ceremony, the bride and groom are accompanied with a procession of boats full of well-wishers who sing and clap to the musician's drumbeat. The sound fills the whole area as other boats join in and hurl flowers along the path of the bride and groom for good luck. The festivity 'sahra' continues until the early hours of the morning and this formal entertainment is a ritual to bring about marital bliss.

Another activity is now regarded with importance. Once a year a special bet race takes place, reserved only for women. They take pride in getting into their traditional canoes and with their oars paddle, in order to win first prize. This is a show of courage and advancement as spectators watch, cheer and bet on the winner.

The various chiefs of the area all assemble under a main grandstand and show great satisfaction when their team wins. This form of amusement distracts, amuses and appeals to an increasing crowd every year.

The people here are superstitious and believe in ways to 'ward off the evil'. If you visit this area with ill intentions, the Ma'dan believe that you will be engulfed by the legendary invisible island called 'Hufaidh'. You will then drown and be swallowed by the serpents.

Wilfred Thesiger describes the island with the following quote from his book 'The Marsh Arabs'.

"On the mythical island are palaces and palm trees and gardens and pomegranates and the buffaloes are bigger than ours. But no one knows exactly where it is, anyone who sees Hufaidh is bewitched and afterwards no one can understand his words. They say the 'Jinns' can hide the island from anyone who comes near it".

"You must understand that seeing is believing but also know that believing is seeing" Denis Waitley

AQAR KOUF ZIGGURAT – You cannot journey into the afterlife with your wealth

During the spring season it was ideal to take short trips and rediscover the archaeological sites.

We drove for about three hours to the city of Abu Ghreb to enhance our knowledge on the history of the Kassite kingdom. These people left a legacy in the midst of the desert for us to explore, a ziggurat which was built in the 14th century by King Kurugalzu I and II. Here amongst a barren landscape rose an empire not to be forgotten.

The Kassite kings ruled the area for nearly four hundred years and glorified themselves as divinities who believed in an afterlife. Thereby they built monuments, temples and palaces. They also established a large city close to the river Euphrates where the fertile land and river silt would yield enough food to sustain the whole Kassite population.

On the relentless quest for life after death, they built a high grandiose staircase which would lead them closer to the heavens. Lush burial chambers encased their bodies. To reach eternal glory they had all the amenities to sustain them as well as immortal treasures lying in the tomb complex next to them. The protective items deposited in the chambers were likely accompanied with magical rituals to pacify their spirits and ensure a safe passage. Texts which were found have revealed facts on their belief in the transition to a better life. Bodies were placed to rest, facing the west, and an opening by the ceilings of the chamber is where they believed that the souls, and then their bodies, would take flight into eternity. All this bears witness that "*you cannot journey into the afterlife with your wealth.*'

Some of the temples have vaulted storage chambers and granaries. They knew that this land was suitable for cultivation so they built an agricultural center, developed an irrigation system and set up trade which made them excel in this region. There was thereby an abundance of corn, vegetables, fruits and minerals.

In the midst of the plateau arises a ziggurat with three flights of steps reaching to the upper levels, (one in front and two on the sides) which lead to a flat roof. This was a shrine for religious festivals with people bringing offerings to their god Enlil, with various processions to thank the deity for the luxuries and the good life that they had attained.

It is encompassed by a temple complex and made of sun-dried bricks interlaced with reed mats and surrounded by a wall. The buildings behind this ziggurat are the palace complexes which were the residences of the royal families. The surrounding ruins may have been the homes of the local people.

This will captivate anyone's imagination because the Kassites did not want their empire to cease to exist. It is an example of their advanced civilization, clearly demonstrating the extent of knowledge and prosperity.

Unfortunately, there are no inscriptions or reliefs on the wall. The only relics found were chiseled stone tablets which shed some light on this shining civilization. They are now displayed in the National Museum of Iraq.

The surviving 'Kudurru' relic is one of the few Kassite surviving artifacts. Engraved on the stone slabs are images on the top with cuneiform script, which describes a binding land contract, a legal account of acquisition of property. A day of knowledge is always beneficial.

"So much of our future lies in preserving the past". *Peter Westbrook.*

CODE OF HAMMURABI-THE WISE RULER WHO INSTITUTED THE RULES OF LAWS - *"Liberty is the right to do what the Law permits"* Charles de Monteqlieu

Hammurabi was the 6th king of Babylon. He desired to establish order in his country and in order to quell unrest he united Mesopotamia. He instituted 282 rules of conduct which were inscribed on a stone monument in the Akkadian language. The monument is now an exhibit at the Louvre in Paris. The replica is displayed on the window panel in Babylon in one of the chambers of Nebuchadnezzar's Royal Palace.

These are the earliest laws recorded in history written on a diorite stele. The seven-foot statue portrays Hammurabi receiving the laws from Shamash, 'the god of justice', who is seen sitting on his throne and holding a scepter in his right hand as a symbol of authority and power. The lower part and the back of the statue bear the laws inscribed in columns. It was believed that Hammurabi was the 'chosen one' worthy of bringing righteousness to his nation.

It was important for his people to conduct themselves in an honorable manner, he wanted a higher quality of life, and his objective was an enforced rule of conduct. His control and comfort would be beneficial in their lives because *"Where there is law, there definitely is order."*

His famous quote was *"The gods called me the exalted prince who feared God, to bring the rule of law in the land, to destroy the wicked and the evil doers so that the strong harm not the weak"*.

He thus managed to establish law abiding citizens as he enforced these codes for social order. If his people violated any of them, they would have had to endure severe punishment and fines.

He had the stele placed in the main square for the public to see and to abide to. Here are some of his codes:

-"If a man has married a wife and a disease has seized her, if he is determined to marry a second wife, he shall marry her. He shall not divorce the wife unto whom the disease has seized. In the home they made together she shall dwell and he shall maintain her as long as she lives".

-"If a man has determined to disinherit his son and has declared before the judge "I cut off my son", the judge shall enquire into the son's past and if the son has not committed grave misdemeanor, the father shall not disinherit the son."

-"If a man has not his witness at hand, the judge shall set him a fixed time not exceeding six months, and if within six months he has not produced his witness the man has then lied, he shall bear the penalty."

-"That the strong might not injure the weak in order to protect the widows and orphans, in order to bespeak justice in the land to settle all disputes and heal all injuries laws of justice intended to clarify the rights of any oppressed man."

The world will always be indebted to King Hammurabi who is classified as one of the twenty-three most famous lawgivers. He is credited with a plaque at the U.S. Supreme Court Building and the U.S. House of Representatives in the Capitol.

EPIC OF GILGAMESH – QUEST FOR IMMORTALITY

Do you believe in immortality as Gilgamesh did?

The oldest texts in architecture are the surviving Sumerian texts which date back to 2,500 B.C. They were found amidst ruins in Ninevah and were unearthed in the library of Assurbanipal, directly from his vaulted rooms.

Gilgamesh was the 4th king of Uruk and was considered a god and a hero. He was fierce and ruthless and suppressed the inhabitants of his land as he wanted to outshine his predecessors and contemporaries.

His people suffered immensely and were in so much distress that they turned to their gods and prayed to find relief and obtain mercy from this ruler. Their lamentations were heard, and an untamed creature named Enkidu was created by the gods sent to annihilate Gilgamesh.

Gilgamesh and Enkidu engage in daily combat, but neither is defeated. Tired of his personal battle, Gilgamesh decides to grant Enkidu mercy, which the latter accepts. Time goes by and peace prevails as a friendship develops between the two enemies. They share a series of adventures. They both overcome dangers and difficulties and arrive to the conclusion that unity is stronger than enmity.

Unfortunately, during one of the escapades, Enkidu gets sick and dies. Gilgamesh is heartbroken and stricken with grief. He is devastated and as fear of death overcomes him, he develops a desire to live forever. He decides to embark on a mission to escape the same fate.

Overwhelmed, he decides to travel throughout the world and seek ways and find answers to the secret of overcoming death. But he yields no success.

He becomes weary of his endless pursuits and is told by the inhabitants of the various cities to return back to his homeland.

But one day he hears about the existence of a wondrous plant which can yield infinite youth and revitalize and rejuvenate mankind. 'The Boxthorn plant' with edible longevity berries. He ventures all around the country and searches high and low until he finds a ferryman called Urshanabi, who directs him to the sea where the magic plant grows.

Gilgamesh attaches heavy stones around his feet, dives into the seas and drags himself down deep. He sees the plant and pulls it from its roots and swims back ashore, feeling satisfied and invincible.

He carries the plant in his hands and heads back home. The journey is long and the weather is sizzling hot, so he decides to bathe by a nearby spring which appears cool and inviting. As he lunges into the water, he accidentally drops the plant, which slips away and gets swallowed by a passing fish.

Gilgamesh despairs and searches frantically everywhere, but by then the fish is nowhere to be found. Feeling helpless and powerless and with sadness in his heart, he heads back to his land distressed. At this point, he renounces and decides to leave his fate in the hands of the gods.

During his lonely journey, he contemplates as to the purpose of these incidents. He realizes that his fight for eternal life can no longer be reality, that it is beyond his power to overcome death.

He then adopts a new concept of life, he learns a good lesson and decides to become a conscientious merciful ruler to his nation. He vows to change his ways extending understanding and consideration for his people.

The twelve oldest surviving fragments in clay tablets, on display in the British Museum in room 55, recount stories of the deluge. The cuneiform script depicts the existence and efforts of trying to find the life giving plant carved on stone to live forever.

Immortality does not exist but it is useful to know that the Boxthorn plant has edible ripe berries with nutritional properties including Vitamin A, B and C as well as Omega 3. It is an anti-oxidant and does strengthen the immune system. This plant is also called the 'matrimony vine' and it is believed to cause disharmony in one's marriage if it is planted in one's garden!

"Immortality is to live your life doing good things and
leaving your mark behind." Callimahus

So you still think that the waters from the fabled fountains of youth will rejuvenate you, or the elixir magic potion will extend your life? For many years researchers and scientists have aimed at reversing the ageing process but still their efforts are fruitless.

So it is best that you enjoy every day of your life as you age. Only by using your anti-ageing wisdom you can improve the quality of your life. Make healthier choices with the food you eat, cook at home, drink a lot of water, consume very little meat and burn the extra calories. Be content by adding a sense of purpose, celebrate life with gratitude daily and devote your life by doing good deeds.

"Age has its own glory, beauty and wisdom that belong to it" Joseph Murphy

SAMARRA – Once the capital of Iraq

In 1975 we took a trip to Samarra, 80 miles north of Baghdad to visit the famous Spiral Tower El Mulwiya. As we drove, we saw from a distance the impressive tower ahead of us. This was the symbol of Samarra. A distinguished landmark which was the pride of this city,

As soon as we reached the spot, we stood in front of the Great Mosque, a structure which resembled a ziggurat, soaring up to a height of several hundred feet. We felt motivated to climb up the outdoor spiral staircase. It was built in a circular fashion. The ramps made of sun-dried bricks lead us to the very top and then took us to a flat platform which offered a panoramic view of the whole town where traces of history remained.

The ascent was pleasant as we were guided with great stories of the city which was once the Islamic capital of Iraq. In the past, a respected official of the mosque would be appointed to climb to the top of the minaret and summon the believers to cease their activities and pray five times a day.

This was once a place of worship, built around the 9th century, by the Abbasid Caliphs which made Samarra their administrative intellectual and religious capital. When we reached the uppermost level, we came to a circular room where we stopped to view our surroundings. You could clearly see the ruins of older mosques and palaces as we took several notes on the life of the various imams who lived here.

Then we descended and headed to the golden dome mosque which shone from afar. It was built in 1905 and was visible from a distance with its two golden minarets. We were told that under the dome lay the tombs of 10th Imam Al Hadi and 11th imam who was his son, Imam Hassan al Askeri. Also here lay the bodies of two females, his sister Hakima Khatoun and his mother Nargis Khatoun. Its intricate architecture and classical style, as well as its gleaming colors, make this mosque unique. We then visited the famous mosque 'Ali Hada El Haskan' which stood majestically in the center of the town. In fact, my whole family as well as my then husband from Italy, could not resist a visit inside this holy site. They were mesmerized by the splendor of the Islamic architecture inside and outside.

The interior hall was a real sanctuary, lit with immense crystal-clear chandeliers and different light fixtures reflecting on the mirrored walls. It was decorated with lapis lazuli, casting sheer bright light in all directions. It was a custom to write out a question on a piece of paper and leave it by the mosque. Your message would be eventually delivered, read, and answered as the Imams would consider your praises, comments and concerns.

Close by, another mosque with a blue dome had inscriptions from the holy Koran with verses hand-calligraphed. The dome and minarets were decorated mainly with blue tiles and mosaics in blue arabesque design. This was where the 12th Imam Muhammad al Mahmi once secretly lived. It was his holy hideout, the only place where he survived the fate of his father who was persecuted by his fierce opponents.

John O'Hara the author of several screenplays and successful short novels was inspired by this city and thereby wrote a book called *"An Appointment in Samarra"*.

"Whoever works righteousness, man or woman, and has faith, verily to them will We give a new life, a life that is good and pure, and We will bestow on them such rewards according to the best of their actions" (Holy Qur'an 16:97).

UR – KINGDOM OF QUEEN PUABI

The Ziggurat of Ur stands steadfast in the midst of the desert close to Nassiriyah. The first skyscrapers in the world. This was a shrine built to honor and worship the patron moon god Nanna and was once a coastal city by the Euphrates which has since then changed its course.

Lord Leonard Woolley, the great English archaeologist developed a strong curiosity about this site and in 1924 decided to excavate the several mounds and discovered many burial chambers.

The dynasty of Queen Puabi ruled this city and forensic tests reveal that she was young of age when she died. She was buried with several attendants along with a variety of funerary goods by her side. The Sumerians believed that there was life after death, so the royalty class was privileged by being laid to rest in the cool chambers of the ziggurat so as to preserve the body longer.

A magnificent box, called 'The Standard of Ur' was also unearthed, which tells a story of the daily lives of the people and depicts their social levels. There are two panels which show the outcome of existence during war and peace. The lower-level side depicts battles with armed soldiers in their chariots trampling over the enemy. Then well-dressed guards leading infantry troops with their spears as they hold on to their captives. Upper-level shows bounty being presented to the king whose royal image is larger than the other people around him. It also shows enslaved detainees whom the army unit present as symbols of victory and triumph.

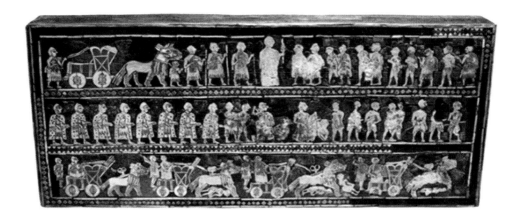

The panel has an image of peace. It shows the laborers bringing abundant supplies of food, and then above that, the herdsmen and farmers of high level presenting their oxen, bulls and sheep and fish. On the top, we see affluence in the empire where there is freedom from battles. It is a tranquil scene with festivity at a banquet. The king and his entourage are celebrating with bounty and music while a musician is playing the lyre accompanied by a vocalist.

Comparing the contrasting scenes illustrates the hardship and suffering in times of conflict and war, pointing out that having peace always brings prosperity and pleasure.

Amongst the treasures found in the tomb was the headdress of the queen, a lyre, a statue of ram in a thicket, a golden chariot, many pieces of jewelry, cylinder seals which carried her name, cosmetics, trinkets, vases and a game board.

To be buried with her riches would ensure her power and wealth. Her status would be recognized, and she would enjoy all the benefits of the afterlife. In addition, she believed that her soul would travel through the portholes, ascend to the heavens and journey from one world to the next, leaving their goods undisturbed. To appease her spirit, ceremonial artifacts were set alongside the body. Rituals and spells were recited to scare away evil spirits for her to continue having an influence in the divine world. She would thereby ascend easily to the heavens.

The stepped Sumerian tower has three platforms with three staircases, one in the center and two flanked on the sides leading to the terraces. On the very top, a flat roof platform was a shrine dedicated to the gods where sacrifices were made. Religious services accompanied by ritual processions were held whereby people brought their offerings and placed them by the vaulted doorways. (Only the priests and scribes were allowed into the complex). They built this temple-stepped tower as a stairway to get closer to heaven. It was their call for salvation, as they believed that their prayers would be heard clearer after their invocation ceremonies. Moreover, the higher the ziggurat, the safer it was for the elite to evade from the destructive rain floods occurring yearly.

The scale of the number of excavations of homes surrounded with winding roads and courtyards show the degree of importance of this site.

This was a major city where wealth and power prevailed, as artifacts together with clay tables in cuneiform deposited in the archives, were emblematic of commercial and political importance.

The historically significant visit by Pope Francis to Iraq, in 2021, was to bring a peaceful co-existence between Shiite, Sunni and Christian religions. Hundreds of Iraqis lined the streets in major cities to welcome the bearer of peace. He came to ask an end to intolerance and to encourage Christians to stay in Iraq to help rebuild this nation. He was greeted with open arms by the Prime Minister Mustafa Al Kadhimi, the President Barham Salih in Baghdad. Then he visited the grand Ayatollah Al Sistini in Najaf. Later he headed to the North Kurdish region. Met with President Nechirvan Barzani and Prime Minister Masour Barzani. He conducted open air masses in Erbil with 10,000 attendees. His last visit was to the Biblical home of Abraham, the Patriarch of Islam, Christian and Jewish religions. A visit well worthwhile for unity.

LAKE HABBANIYA

There will never be a shortage of water at Lake Habbaniya. One of the tributaries of the Euphrates River replenishes this natural lake. It is a perfect getaway from the city life.

This was our ideal spot for a weekend. Habbaniya is only 58 miles from the capital. This favorite destination was merely a shallow natural fresh water lake used for recreational purposes. We would go early to find a tranquil spot by the open beach to set up our picnic gear. We rented a bungalow surrounded by lush lawns and swimming pools with shaded avenues ornate with groomed gardens.

The Royal Air Force of England set up base here. The British airfield was stationed and became operational from 1938 until 1959. Habbaniya was an ideal airfield since it was completely flat and was perfect for the flying training exercises.

In 1950's the British Mandate set up both an airbase and an airfield, together with their headquarters and a sailing club. They eventually transformed the area into a picturesque resort with tennis courts and swimming pools. The charm always remained and although the area remained isolated for a few years, it still retained its appeal with its fairgrounds and shaded parks as it attracted large crowds on the weekends.

The panoramic large waterfront hotel was crowded with foreign visitors for weddings and honeymoons. It had discotheques, restaurants and music bars. It became a vibrant town with many recreational activities including beach clubs, golf courses, cruising and water skiing.

We would enjoy our meals, make new friends and go swimming. Since these waters were navigable, we were enthused by seeing many boats passing by. Then we would all sit and watch the sunset with its beautiful yellow orange rays as we sipped tea and coffee. Later we headed to our bungalow for the evening, as our parents and adult family members went out.

There is a beautiful saying in Arabic: "*Do a good deed and then lunge it in the water and expect something good to happen in return, some day.*"

'Remembrance Day' is still celebrated to honor the 280 British service members of Royal Air Force who are buried here, as this was a major military base and flying training center with barracks, hotels, swimming pools and bazaars.

This tourist village with its wide beaches and sparkling blue water, its palm trees and once well-groomed lawns will reclaim its glory. It will become a luxurious holiday resort for its people and its visitors again, just like it used to be.

"A man travels the world over in search of what he needs
and returns home to find it!" George Moore

KIRKUK NORTHERN IRAQ

Kirkuk is classified as one of the oldest cities in the world. It is the center of the petroleum industry and is rich with oil fields reserves and pipelines which run to ports on the Mediterranean Sea. It is a fertile area where large farmlands are cultivated. Because of its ethnically mixed inhabitants, it has gone through turbulent times since the Arabs, Kurds and Turks & Assyrians each claim this region to be theirs. It stands on the site of ancient Assyria close to the foothills of the beautiful Zagros Mountains. The Assyrian Empire survived for centuries and the many Christian Assyrians still live in the northern part of Iraq, Nineveh, close to Mosul. Their ancient city of Nineveh was on the eastern part of Upper Tigris and was the largest city of the neo-Assyrian empire.

The capital was Ashur with entryways to the city through the 'Nergal Gate'. It still stands proudly and shows towering strength over the area. The human headed winged bull sculptures at the entry of the palaces now stand in the National Museum of Iraq and Louvre Museum in France. They are evidence of the grandeur of their kings Ashurbanipal II, Sargon II, and Sennacherib.

In the 1930's, the palace of Ashurbanipal was discovered along with the throne room and several chambers containing literary wealth. Thousands of tablets written in cuneiform script are now exhibited in the museum.

Kirkuk had a pleasant mild climate and I remember my father taking me on his motorcycle for a ride and showing me the vast parks, green hills and pleasant meadows. One could not imagine that the vast hot desert lay just a few miles away. It was a pleasant place where we enjoyed our little villa facing an evergreen steep hill.

An important note about the discoveries of Calouste Sarkis Gulbenkian in this area is worth mentioning. He was an oil magnate and a very smart man who saw a great potential in this land. He was an Armenian engineer who envisioned and developed prosperity. Gulbenkian was a businessman from a merchant family who believed in exploring crude oil reserves in this area. His powers of observation and his skill as a petroleum engineer empowered him to face several challenges to detect new petroleum sites. He would convince the government to fund projects and to give him the oil exploration rights to drill more oil wells. He became one of the wealthiest people of the 20th century as a result of converting ideas into money. Subsequently he was nicknamed 'Mr. Five Percent' because that was the percentage of shares he requested and gained for his purposeful effort. He was a man who had no fear of any failure and possessed a great desire to achieve success and ready to surmount any difficulty. He was diligent in his work and had the drive and energy to make efforts and convince people to trust him.

He also built a grand outdoor stadium for the Iraqis. After his success in Iraq, Gulbenkian ventured to Lisbon, Portugal where he became an avid art and sculpture collector. He dedicated his last years to forming a foundation called 'Calouste Gulbenkian Foundation' which is still a charitable institution and exhibition gallery. The renowned center with large gardens, terraced ground with a pond and fountains has a vast treasure of Islamic, Greek, Roman, Egyptian, and European art.

Subsequently, I believe that if the wealth of my nation would be divided fairly and honestly, each and every Iraqi would become a millionaire.

"Better a small piece of a big pie than a big piece of a small pie" Gulbenkian.)

HATRA - Al Hadr- Once an Oasis City – In the barren landscape once rose an empire

The city of Hatra greeted you with her statues of guardian goddesses Tische and Fortuna. It is situated about 186 miles from Baghdad. The major divinities were a testimony of development and progress. They opened the gates to a significant archaeological site. It is presently proclaimed as a World Heritage Site by UNESCO (United Nations Educational Scientific & Cultural Organization).

Columns, arched temples, shrines and sculptures are found here. The city was first classified as a desert settlement, but the diversity of its inhabitants and their wisdom transformed the place into a major cultivated trading center.

This was also a religious place dedicated to several deities. A place of worship, where rituals were performed during the Parthian dynasty. It was a sanctuary where a man-made lake was set up for ceremonial cleansing. The shrines where the religious functions were performed still stand. Fortification walls with four gates surrounded the circular city. It was a fortress city built to withstand and survive various invasions, specifically by the Romans. It contained two walls with an inner insurmountable moat.

Amongst old records, you will find Roman emperors such as Severus and Trajan mentioning their unaccomplished siege against a city that had the best defense system and manned by strong willed people.

The architecture of the city is eclectic as it includes Parthian, Roman, Greek and Assyrian as well as Arabic styles. Inscriptions denote 'King Sanantruq' as the King of Arabs and his father 'Nasr' as the great priest during the Arab dynasty. Prosperity grew fast and flourished thanks to the trade route established here. The Hatrene merchants exchanged their valued merchandise such as silk, spices, gems and carpentry and transported it on the Tigris to Syria and to other mid-eastern countries all the way to Europe. Various inscriptions were found dating back to 140 A.D., which testify to the splendor of this city.

When the Sassanids came to power, they destroyed and abandoned the city. But the ruins remain and the local people, who are all related, are hopeful that Hatra will once again be a major tourist spot and will allow us to unravel its intriguing past.

Unfortunately, part of this site was blown up by aggressors. A complete loss to this civilization and humanity because by destroying the past, they have destroyed their future. In addition, an imposing reminder is that they have left an angry mark in the dormant sands of time. The spirits which dwell in the grains have captured a picture of their wrongdoings and conveyed a clear message to eventually punish those who have done wrong.

"God sees it all"

BASRAH – CITY OF 'SINDBAD THE SAILOR'

Sindbad of the 1,001 Nights Tales set sail from Basrah, his favorite city, on his mysterious seven challenging and wondrous voyages.

He managed to survive all the difficulties and danger of his journeys and discovered great wealth upon his return home. His motto was never to return "*empty handed*".

The' Island of Sindbad' has a gambling casino, 'Casino Tesstahil' (translates to: 'you deserve it'). This is a beach resort island, an escape from daily life, and a place which attracts many tourists from abroad. it hosts many forms of entertainment to visitors.

It was well known also because of hosting various Arabic and European artists and providing a thrill with gambling, somehow following the footsteps of Sindbad, who would bestow them good fortune.

The coastal city of Basrah is a very different place than the other cities of Iraq. It is surrounded with waterways and canals and situated in southern Iraq by the Shatt el Arab where several ports were set up. A new program is underway to clean up all the waterways.

This is a gateway to the sea and to the whole world. It became a popular tourist destination since it attracted people from the neighboring countries. The city was alive both daytime and nighttime.

At dusk, scores of people would go for a seaside promenade on the waterfront boulevards. They socialized and enjoyed the nightlife scenery. The outdoor cafes and restaurants, rooftop eateries and modern hotels including the Sheraton, The Arabian

Gulf Hotel and Novotel rendered the city vibrant, as lights glimmered all along the harbor front. Families were present at the amusement parks, namely 'The Andalusian Park' and 'Luna Park' situated in the public gardens.

At night, it was customary to sit by the shores of the bay and watch the boats glide by. The younger crowd mingled peacefully in Basrah, which was a liberated place. Women wore up to date fashionable western clothes and socialized with their men friends.

Everybody had a job in Basrah, either at the ports, in the petroleum industry or agricultural fields as the rich soil in this area made cultivation very productive. There was work for everyone, as Basrawis were known to be always eager to improve themselves and work hard in any field that was available. Thereby there was immediate growth and prosperity, which was the norm of the day.

It is worthwhile to mention the dormant part of the oldest section of the city, as an important aspect of architecture stands out here. The mid twentieth century "shanasheels" were special verandahs built usually on the upper floors of homes. These balconies jutted out of the rooms and had lattice wooden screens, which opened up like windows. It was not appropriate for women to sit on the balconies, so the screens provided privacy. Women did not have many outlets; this was the way they could see the outside world but the outside world could not see them.

The shutters were made of Cedar wood used for absorbing humidity, block insects and provide protection from the hot sun. They also allowed the faint sea breeze to drift through the openings.

Legend says that some women who felt confined to their homes and isolated from the real world, felt sheltered by the lattice wood screens. They would sit on their windowsills and find solace in singing melodically, in hopes that the birds and the breeze would carry the messages of longing to the world nearby. Their hope was that their wishes of freedom would be heard and answered one day.

Now life is changing and the traditional 'shanasheels' are part of the houses which now belong to history.

The Shatt el Arab region, where the Tigris and Euphrates meet, was a route to Southeast Asia and China. The famous quote by Jahiz says: *"Our sea is worth all the others put together for there is no other unto which God has put so many blessings, it flows into the Indian Ocean which extends for an unknown distance and carries fortune for everyone"*.

This reminds me of the time of leisure in my life. In the evenings to catch cooler breeze, we sat on the second-floor balcony in Bab el Shargi in Baghdad since we had a beautiful view of Umma Gardens in front of our house. The huge public park was alive with lots of people walking or sitting on the benches and the lights in every corner of the large fountain were a sheer delight. In order to do this, we had to draw a curtain on our balcony's lower railing for privacy. It was a habit that we became accustomed to, so as to avoid public stare of men.

Life now has changed.

ADAM'S TREE AT GARDEN OF EDEN – QURNA – South Iraq

Adam's Tree is believed to be one of the oldest, everlasting trees on this land, located on a site which was once known as the Garden of Eden. It is named 'the tree of knowledge' and many people come from faraway places to pray here. Worshippers trust the power it holds to heal illnesses and hundreds of ill visitors arrive visit this spot. A large inscription panel describes its history.

Sightseers are not allowed to eat the fruit from this tree, nor cut off any branches or take any of the fallen twigs. They can, however, make a wish and tie a green ribbon around the closest branch as they make their request.

At this site one has to reflect and absorb productive thoughts and feelings which empower the soul and dissipate negativity. The force which lies in this tree generates a mystifying protective aura as vibrations flow from its branches to individuals in order to overcome temptation and setbacks.

This tree is in Qurna, which lies adjacent to the confluence of the Tigris and Euphrates rivers, is near Basrah. The city has large farmlands as well as a large production center for palm groves due to the rich soil and sunny weather, allowing the easy growth of all types of vegetation. Hence, it is believed this fertile area to have been the 'Garden of Eden'. *"Eden was in Iraq"* Genesis 2:10

THE MAGIC TREE OF LIFE -"That which makes life worth living"

Under the mounds in Nimrud in Ashurbanipal's palace sculptured reliefs on walls portraying *The Tree of Life* were found. Winged High Priests with falcon masks are seen in a spiritual approach, anointing the Pomegranate tree with a cone held in one hand, clenching a bag in the other. The muscular robust men, in ceremonial outfits, are engaged in a divination ritual, reciting prayers, chanting praise to ensure plentiful harvest. They believed that as high priests, they possessed divine power to create a magical remedy for survival, in which the nutrients would extend their lives and improve the quality of a healthy existence.

This yearly ceremony of life amplified their belief in nature's wonders. The budding of the blossoms of the tree, shows the sign of the arrival of spring, the time to venerate the spirits dwelling therein. The edible *fruit of life* would yield an anti-ageing substance of nutritional value, with medicinal properties to promote longevity. Pomegranate seeds are a dietary fiber, contain protein, omega 6, antioxidant, vitamin B and C and promote good health to combat infection.

It is beneficial to add that there also exists the 'Artemisia' perennial evergreen herb shrub which has its own medicinal properties. It relieves menstrual cramping, improves digestive disorders, and acts as a liver tonic.

People nowadays believe in the energy trees possess, and one technique to release negative energy is to place the palms of your hand and rest your forehead on the trunk of a tree then hug the tree. Close your eyes, relax, and feel connected to the positive flow from the tree to your body that filters through with positive frequencies. Release all negative thoughts. You will feel connected and there will occur an exchange of force with a virtuous cleansing transformation.

MOSUL

Mosul is another important city in the northern part of Iraq, about 250 miles north from Baghdad. It is called the city of two Springs. The summers are milder, and the weather is pleasant during spring and autumn as it is situated close to the Zagros Mountains.

Mosul is renowned for it is the place where cotton 'muslin' was first produced in the Middle East. The name derives from this city originally called Mosulian and became famous for its quality. Thanks to long pleasant seasons, cotton plants grew in abundance and its manufacture and trade enabled good prospects for its people.

'Al Kabeer Nouri Mosque' is well known because of its 'leaning minaret' and the city also had a great museum surrounded with modern hotels Rafidain Hotel and Al Mahaliya Hotel.

Spring festivals were held annually in April when hundreds of floats overflowing with multi colorful vibrant blossoming flowers from the region cruised through the main thoroughfares. They would leave behind the air heavy with the scent of flowers and once again livened Mosul as this was the time where tourists flowed into this city to admire the gifts of nature.

Some interesting sites include 'Qara Sarai' – The Black Palace. The castle of Bash Tabiya which comprises the ancient walls of Mosul city dating back to 12 century, Mosul Museum, the Mausoleum of Imam Yahya Abil Qasim and the ancient Chaldean churches, as well as the Monasteries of Mar Gurgis and Mar Behnam.

It has been the center of commerce and communications as its roads create a link to the east with Syria, Turkey and Europe, through which the 'Orient Express' passes.

CITADEL IN ERBIL KURDISTAN CAPITAL – NORTHERN IRAQ - On top of a mound is the famous citadel which is classified as the oldest fortress in the world. It rises about 120 feet and the circular outer walls are the actual walls of homes built along the peripheral enclosure.

The statue of Mubarak Ahmed Ibn Mustawfi greets you at the entrance by the gateway of the citadel. He is absorbed in his books and is gratified by the flow of visitors. He is an intellectual who had written several volumes about the history and culture of his beloved city of Erbil. The image denotes the importance of education and acquiring knowledge. He is opening up the doors to allow the world to comprehend the significance of rediscovering the ancient life traditions of this site (which is classified as one of the oldest inhabited cities in the world).

The four different sections are comprised of three hundred houses with public buildings, mansions, schools and Mulla Effendi Mosque which still stand amongst a labyrinth of alleys. The Textile Museum has been set up in one of the old traditional elite homes owned by a famous merchant. It includes hand woven carpets and rugs and runners, bags, hats, textile artifacts and household furniture.

On the left-hand side is the Antique Kala Shop which sells souvenirs, a wide array of books and maps and postcards which outline the 3,000-year history of the citadel and its surroundings. Although most of the older sections have been sealed off because they are all being restored, it is still very satisfying to visit this locality because of its antiquity, architecture and history. You can also enjoy the beautiful panoramic view of the Shar Garden Square with its innumerable lit fountains and sprawling affluent city.

This citadel has its own unique character and while it rests on top of the hill, it stands out significantly and will soon be classified as a World Heritage Site by Unesco. This site attracts many visitors and tourists and there is an unprecedented growth in this region. Foreign investors flock in to build new hotels and shopping malls in Erbil.

NORTHERN IRAQ – A magnetism for tourists

Did you even know such a picturesque, beautiful place existed in Iraq? Agatha Christie, the famous mystery writer, was infatuated by Iraq and Syria. The archaeological excavations gave Christie and her husband insight about the ancient sites in Mesopotamia and so they wanted the world to know about their personal experiences. She consequently wrote several novels inspired by her personal memories. One famous quote of hers about Kurdistan is:" There *can be, I think, no spot in the world so beautiful, so peaceful with the trees and pomegranates, following a mountain stream air is fresh, clear and blue, all is calm and gentle and peaceful here. There are gentle faced custodians bringing you refreshments and you sit in perfect peace while sipping tea"*.

On their way, Christie and her husband went on an expedition to visit the shrine of Sheikh Adi at Lalik, situated a few miles from Mosul, where they were intrigued by the

Yazidi pilgrims who prayed and performed ancient ritual observances at this religious epicenter. So now it is your turn to discover an entirely amazing different landscape, a panorama of green lush surroundings and spectacular colorful sceneries of the Zagros Mountains. Nostalgia floats through my mind as I remember the extensive valleys with the sea of endless colors, eternal woods, blue streams, and gushing waterfalls.

It seems to be hidden from the world but in reality, this is the ideal summer destination ideal vacation spot visited by hundreds and thousands of people. The number continues to grow as the world awakens to its existence.

Many of our ideal summer days were spent in Shaklawa as I reminisce about the sweet scent in the air and the beauty of green meadows which surrounded us.

This is Kurdistan, where the Kurds live in harmony and peace. They are Indo European people with their own distinctive language. Everyone feels safe here and the place is getting more and more famous as time goes by.

My family would rent a chalet and we would dine in the restaurants by the waterfalls. On other days we would head for picnics to the green fields exploding with colorful wildflowers. Music was in the air as my brother strummed on his guitar and my cousins played on their hand-held drums. Serenity ruled while the people picnicking nearby invited us to join them.

This is a 'haven' for visitors because of the stability, security and great economic growth. There is an increase in the number of high-rise buildings, hotels, malls, villas and businesses with daily improvement and agricultural expansion.

The Kurds are very passionate about their land and dedicated to their culture, and this is why we learned to honor these mountains while people here breathe the elements of peace.

When winter came, the Zagros Mountains were covered in shining white velour snow where you could go skiing and snowboarding or take a snow lift to admire the spectacular panorama.

MONASTERIES IN NORTHERN IRAQ

Rabban Hormizd Chaldean Monastery situated a few miles from Alqosh (Mosul) is a city where most Chaldean and Assyrian Christians have dwelt for centuries.

Here the monks led a solitary and restricted life in an isolated community where they took religious vows to be obedient, disciplined, while abstaining from world pleasures. They were committed to the Lord and renounced to wealth. They believed in peace while they resided in simple cells. Their days were dedicated to prayer as they studied the scriptures and recited liturgy with an aim towards religious and spiritual teachings.

A paved path leads you to the church. It is roughly chiseled into the stone slopes of the mountains. Shaded in a maroon color, it has a great number of caves carved into the rocks with no doors or windows. Alcoves around the halls are cells which may have been the sleeping quarters of the monks. They can be reached through tight terraces.

These monks led a simple life and depended on the crops they grew. They collected rainwater and stored it in cisterns as this was their sole beverage. They had no electricity or modern appliances. When the bells rang, they congregated for prayer several times a day.

During Christmas and New Year as well as Easter, the monasteries receive many visitors. Here, people find solace and get to appreciate the simple things in life. A new monastery has now been built a few miles away on a pleasant mountainous location.

St. Elijah Monastery is worth mentioning too. This Assyrian Christian spot is about 6 miles from Mosul and was an important religious center for many Christians. It was founded by Mar Elias Assyrian monks in 6th century but was attacked by Persians in 1744. It was then burned down. It is said that a huge library full of Holy Scriptures was destroyed as the monks were annihilated. When their bodies were discovered by the local people, priests were called in but for fear of reprisal, they had only one place to conceal them, solely in the standing walls. Nowadays the walls are disintegrating in some areas and one can actually see the bones still protruding out of the wall, which is thought of as a good omen.

The tranquil setting has been renovated and includes various halls and rooms, underground tunnels and natural spring water cisterns. At a certain time during the day, beams of light shed a bright glow on the entry halls and walls from a small opening on the ceiling.

As the waters flow steadily from the springs, they are considered to be beneficial and have therapeutic healing properties according to many historical accounts. People of all religions have rediscovered this place and Catholic chaplains now celebrate mass there with escorted tours.

The famous Catherine Monastery on the foothills of Mount Sinai are where Greek Monks reside. It is also worth mentioning this is where the 'Burning Bush' of Moses is replanted in the courtyard. It is a famous place, open to the public only three days a year, as thousands of people visit this site.

"I prefer you to make mistakes in kindness than work
miracles in unkindness" Mother Theresa

Aren't you fascinated with the resources about ancestry which help you rediscover historical records and give you access to search for your ancestors?

In my case as an Armenian, if I were to search for Donikian or Manougian, my own family members, the answer will be "*Census Records not found*" because it would be impossible to trace them. They are amongst the one and a half million Armenians who were massacred by the Ottoman Turks in the years 1915-1918.

I thirst for knowledge about their lives, how advantageous it would be to obtain historical records and documents as well as photos and gather facts about their lives. I would be able to make a connection and would feel pride and a sense of happiness to be capable to build a complete family history.

Now I have to narrow my search exclusively by what my parents have narrated. Below is the story that covers evidence of the suffering of Armenian children and in this case that of my grandfather Donik and his brother Avedis.

Donik and Avedis recounted the sorrowful experience of their escape from Diyabakir eastern Turkey, and the ordeal of walking through the hot torrid desert with their mother and father. They were forcefully deprived of their parents as they were killed by the local police. One night in Haredan Diyarbakir they hid, and they escaped towards the desert. Days of agony filled with thirst and hunger did not stop them from travelling a long distance as they ran for their lives. Extremely tired and worn out, they slept in the desert sand and one morning they noticed from afar a group of Bedouin Arab tents.

They were picked up by the Arab tribesmen who saved them. They accompanied them to another location where there were numerous other camps and discovered other Armenian children who had been rescued.

In the morning, the tribes diverted their routes, the brothers were mounted on separate camels and on that day, my grandfather Donik sorrowfully lost trace of his brother.

My grandmother Azniv and her cousin Vartiter were 12 years of age and their entire family was also massacred but the children managed to find refuge with a Turkish family. As soon as night fell, they were forced to flee towards the Syrian Desert and hand in hand, through tribulations and hunger and thirst, they were picked up one morning by the Arab tribesmen.

In the meantime, Archbishop Moushegh Seropian (Mesopotamian Iraqi Iraq Prelate) was informed about the status of the refugees, so he set up a campaign with British Commander General Austin and his team to immediately come to the rescue. They organized and prepared innumerable number of tents in Baquba Iraq 'Camp Baquba'.

They found out the locations where thousands of children and refugees were situated with the Arab Tribes and set up meetings to pick them up and relocate them to these shelters. Thereby thousands were saved. We owe our thanks to them.

Years later In Mosul, my grandfather managed with the help of Arab tribesmen to find his brother. He helped him get employed at Ain Zaleh Oil Company as an 'oil field man'. He liked his new life but as time went by he missed his family and thus decided to return back to the tribe.

The Armenian Genocide must be recognized by the world and facts as well as documents, films and books reveal the truth. Twenty nations have acknowledged the occurrences and brutal inhumane treatments of the Armenians under the rule of these evil perpetrators: Mehmet Talaat Pasha: Minister of Interior- Enver Pasha: War Minister and leader of Young Turks, Djemal Pasha: Leading military advisor of Young Turks.

The regime was to systematically exterminate the Christian population by deporting them forcibly away from their homes, deprive them of their possessions, march them to the nearby desert and let them perish there. It is witnessed that the troops robbed their homes, raped their women and slaughtered the children in front of the families

Theodore Roosevelt classified the Armenian suffering as: *"The greatest crime of the war"*.

Ambassador Henry Morgentau wrote his memoirs as he witnessed the genocide" Morgenthau's Story" (1918). He spoke about the condition of Armenians and informed higher officials that the same brutal treatments were extended towards the Greeks and Assyrians also living in Turkey. He exasperated since no help was in sight from abroad; he resigned from the post and described "Ottoman Turkey as a *"place of horror"*.

Giacomo Gorrini, Italian Diplomat Consul in Trabzon denounced the genocide, recounted to the press the slaughter he had seen and gave interviews all around the world. He had to take action, so for 20 years he helped thousands of Armenians to depart from Turkey and head to Italy. His book states that *"The Armenians should regain their homeland"*.

George Horton, consul, and journalist, explains in his biography 'The Blight of Asia' from 1926, the ethnic cleansing by the Ottoman Turks as they burned the whole city of Smryna together with the entire Greek and Armenian Christian inhabitants.

The despair led many of the people listed above to organize a relief organization called ACRNE, which was a campaign set up to save the "Starving Armenians". It was founded in 1915 and a fund was set up to gather and distribute money to the missionaries and embassies in Constantinople where more than 140,000 orphans were saved and set up in camps, clinics, shelters and then sent abroad.

As the power of the Ottoman Empire declined, resources and money became scarce and their debt was overwhelmingly high. The British army in 1918 destroyed their armies whilst the three criminals: Talaat Pasha, Enver Pasha,Djemal Pasha fled to Germany.

The Armenian people have <u>no hate</u> towards the Turkish people since they were also forced to obey the laws or endure severe punishments if they were ever caught helping the Armenians. I am happy to say I have a good relationship with my Turkish friends and our worlds never collide.

The new Sultan Mehmed VI was named the head of the new Turkish government and upon recognizing what the Ottomans had done, he courts martialed and sentenced the three Pashas to death. Also a special recognition goes to Governor Mehmet Celal Bey who did whatever he could. He saved hundreds of thousands of Armenians and stood bravely in defiance to the Ottomans. He appealed and supplicated for the end of the deportations, but he was ignored and then removed from his post. His words were: "*Armenian blood was flowing in the river and thousands of innocent children, irreproachable old people, helpless women, strong young men were streaming down this river towards oblivion. Anyone I could save with my bare hands I saved, and the others, they just streamed down the river never to return.*"

Also recognition goes to Cemil Bahri Konne an Ottoman Officer who also rescued and saved hundreds of Armenians. We salute them both.

Subsequently the **Treaty of Sevres**, 'a peace treaty' was signed by four Allies: Britain, France, Italy and Japan. They imposed, liquidated and divided the empire into several nations. The partitioning and the defining of new borders created an Armenian republic nation in Southwest Russia.

Article 88 defined the borders of a new Armenia and thereby Turkey in accordance with the action already taken by Allied Powers, had to recognize Armenia as a free independent state.

King Sharif Ali Bin Hussein Hijaz Father of King Faisal of Iraq who was the leader of the' Arab Revolt', aimed to liberate Arab lands from the Turkish rule and resented the Young Turks, so he issued the following decree: "*To the Hashemite Royal Court and to all Arabs. Help the Armenian community and refugees, let them settle on this land and be good to them and treat them well and protect them, defend them, provide them with anything they need, as if they are one of your own people.*"

This very important decree still hangs in the rectory of the Armenian Orthodox Church, Sourp Krikor Lousavoritch – Al Jadiriyah in Baghdad. His son had the same kind of sentiments towards Armenians.

So we were granted a land to live on peacefully and we remain faithful friends of the Arabs with whom we live in peace.

In Armenian families, we are taught to respect and honor the government in any nation we live in.

Also of mention is the large famous Armenian Memorial Museum and Exhibition Center stands in Yerevan Armenia to honor the victims with an eternal flame that will burn forever in remembrance.

Also of mention is the 'Armenian Orphan Carpet', which is the symbol of salvation. It took one whole year to be completed. It was woven by young orphan girls who survived the genocide and later presented to President Calvin Coolidge in 1925 as a token of appreciation for the Near East Relief who rescued them. Ambassador Henry Morgentau created a charity called 'American Committee for Armenian and Syrian Relief 'to salvage as many children as possible. He mentioned, *"each one of those knots in the carpet was made by a child who lost their parents during the genocide"*. This richly detailed carpet now remains tucked away in the White House.

"Never ever boast yourself up on the back of others sufferings."

ALADDIN'S LAMP

In our living room, we had a beautiful ornament; a copper lamp, which we believed, was magical. Since it was positioned on a shelf in front of the sun, it continuously glowed from every angle of the room and was similar to Aladdin's Lamp from the enchanting tales of 1,001 Arabian Nights.

My brother and I were told as children that a gentle genie resided inside who had the power to master our destiny and make our wishes come true.

We trusted in the genie's famous words from the story "*Your wish is my command*" and we were told to be respectable and honorable in life as well as grateful so as to be worthy of having our wishes fulfilled.

We would hold the lamp, close our eyes and allow good positive thoughts to flow in whilst we cleared our mind, blocked negative thoughts and focused in silence. We then made a wish, which we consciously envisioned and believed as we rubbed our hand against the lamp.

We were told, "*You cannot visibly invoke the noble genie but your thoughts have been sent out since your intentions are good, thereby the genie has heard you and will slowly process and fulfill what you desire whilst good fortune is provided*".

MAKE A WISH

Without skepticism, we were optimistic and believed in the force that lay within the genie and it was evident that we could attract whatever our heart desired. The forces that were around us would bestow our wishes.

When your life gets dull and dreary, change your thinking patterns, shift your thoughts, and bring back the magic luster. Embrace the beauty life has to offer by anticipating better days as you will project confidence. A polished person is an accomplished person with a high degree of refinement who always fits well and is lustrous in society.

Now make a wish.

Allow me now to share my experiences beyond Iraq, to my favorite spots in to **Lebanon** and **Italy**.

BIENVENU AU LIBAN – WELCOME TO LEBANON – SWITZERLAND OF THE MIDDLE EAST

Lebanon is blessed with the Mediterranean Sea, the mountains and streams. Cedar pine forests with up-to date cities as well as mountain villages. A real ' Paradis Terrestre'.

We would go to Broumanna, a 13 miles journey from Beirut. Up to the mountains, through winding roads, we would reach a picturesque spot. The Hotel Florida. We cherished every minute we spent there. During the daytime we had our breakfast and went for long walks through the modern town, its many stores packed with whatever your heart desired. We crossed over to the cedar forests, trying to capture the spicy resinous scent and aroma whilst admiring the breathtaking panorama of Beirut in the distance as well as its blue crystal water of the sea. *"Behold I will liken you to a cedar in Lebanon with fair branches and forest shade" Ezekiel 31:3*

In the evenings, we went to the open-air restaurants, which also offered spectacular majestic views with colorful lights flickering everywhere.

We enjoyed the mezzes, which Lebanon is famous for, truly a feast for the eyes. A vast array of more than 15 dishes beautifully arranged on the table. All the restaurants were packed, and there usually was live music to listen to.

By the time the second serving came, we were already full and when the time came, people got up and began to dance, solo, or hand in hand in a round circle. You could sense the excitement of the crowds, as everyone was there to enjoy themselves without a single worry in their minds.

Here we could wear whatever we wanted and feel completely at ease. During the day we would head to the seaside resorts and preferred St. George Hotel with its vast beaches. Then we went shopping on Hamra Street, Ras Beirut, Asshrafiah with its luxurious shops. It was the fashion scene where Lebanese women and men were dressed very fashionably. Merchandise from all over the world was available.

The 'land of the Phoenicians' leaves an ancient wisdom lying in the ruins of Baalbeck, fifty-four miles away from the capital, in the fertile Bekaa valley, 'The city of the sun' offers an international and impressive festival The Phoenicians venerated their god and dedicated the temple complex to their deity 'Baal'.

Amidst the columns of the Temple of Jupiter, flanked by the Lebanon Mountains, we would attend the most remarkable folklore shows. The whole area came alive, illuminated with interchangeable multicolored floodlights, live music and a show which was incomparable. More than sixty thousand people a year visit this site because of extraordinary stage festival held amongst the colonnade, columns and sculptures.

Jeita Grotto in Lebanon is the most impressive cave in the world. It is still stunning and has remained vivid in my memory. On one of our trips, we headed to the famous tourist site from Beirut. We parked our car and took the train ride to the site, then boarded one of the row boats which serenely flowed in the river Nah El Kalb, accompanied with a guide.

As we entered into the grotto through the underground river over crystalline waters, I remained completely enchanted as if under a hypnotic spell, surrounded by silence. It seemed unreal to explore the marvels of the colorful limestone formations and sculptures formed by Mother Nature. I was amidst a beautiful natural landscape as I admired each stalactite and stalagmite, column and mushroom formation, artistically illuminated with innumerable powerful colorful spotlights.

Every formation, pattern and shape was inspiring. My world came to a standstill amidst an underground paradise. It was an amazing wonderland and I felt that I could not let a moment go by without examining every formation, as I felt that my surroundings had a story to tell as to how it was fashioned. They were carved by master designers of water and time. I wished I could freeze time for a while and admire the ornamented remarkable art gallery, which continues to work its spell on visitors who remain under its hypnotic trance.

Later we were accompanied to the upper level to take a walking tour on the suspended long walkways, which led to the tunnels. Here we had an excellent overview of the cavern and even then, I left in admiration as I watched the great number of tourists leaving in awe, unwilling to budge from their balcony spots. We then went to the souvenir shops and bought several books, postcards and photos as a reminder of this magical spot.

It is of no wonder that this grotto was nominated as one of the 28 finalists in the competition entitled 'The New Seven Wonder of Nature', chosen by people all over the world through an international poll as well as judges based in Switzerland. Nowadays people enjoy the cable car rides which soar over the scenic green Lebanon Mountains offering stunning views. You also have the choice of watching film clips of the entire grotto at the theater on this site. People experience one marvel after another at this genuine intact natural underground art gallery where I believe invisible magicians continue to work their spell of splendor.

By the entrance of the lower cave, you are greeted by a huge statue of the 'Guardian of Time' who tenaciously sits on a fountain lower cave. He seems frozen in time, yet he has a smile on his face which expresses delight in welcoming hundreds and thousands of visitors. He is seated with an outstretched left arm and his beard and long hair locks give him a serene look which expresses that time will never erase what nature has created. He remains solidified to forever preserve, protect and safeguard these caves. During the summer season, special concerts and film presentations take place inside the grotto as it remains captivating, fascinating and delightful, the 'pride of Lebanon.'

Now let's fly and visit '**San Lazzaro Degli Armeni' in Italy-Venice**

Island and its Library

Amidst the tranquil lagoon in Italy, faith floats through the waves on the serene island of San Lazzaro. In 1970's we went to visit the monastery, the home of the Mekhitarist Armenian Catholic monks, and pleasantly greeted by Father Esoian who was our guide.

We took the ferryboat and the moment we stepped on the island, it felt like being on an oasis of peace, far from the chaos of tourists. Father Esoian delved into history and explained how the founder, Father Mekhitar, had to flee with other monks from the Turkish persecutions in 1715 and was saved and brought to Venice with several other monks. Here he showed his faith and dedication and managed to meet with the government rulers who sympathized with his cause since Venice also had a history of prolonged war and conflict with the Ottoman rulers.

Because of the tragic stories of what he and his family and friends went through during the genocide and also his intense Christian faith and his purpose to introduce a new academic lifestyle for study and worship, and desire to set up a publishing center, the Venetian Governor and his associates assigned to him an uninhabited island as a refuge and educational center.

The deserted island of lepers, was to become their new home. With the help of wealthy Armenians and Italians and their donations, the old church was restored; the vast gardens were replenished with fresh flowers and trees while a monastery and a center of culture and publishing house were all set up. The island was thereby restored to life and named Saint Lazzaro Degli Armeni after St. Lazarius the Patron Saint of Lepers.

We passed through the cloister and colonnades, the various galleries of paintings, the museum containing an Egyptian sarcophagus and a real 'Mummy'. There was also a Holy Qur'an, American Indian relics, old Armenian religious items and the library with thousands of Armenian and International translated manuscripts.

As we walked towards the courtyard, we were led to the gardens where roses were artfully planted and prized. The beautiful exhibit of multi-colored roses and the delightful subtle fragrances conveyed a message of serenity. These flowers symbolized warmth, beauty and sweetness and I found out that each color had its own significance. Red was the symbol of enduring love, white was purity, yellow was happiness, pink was gentleness. So while you find yourself on this island, you literally have to 'stop and smell the roses'.

I felt a sense of gratitude for the gifts of nature and saw delight in the faces of the visitors as they listened to the stories narrated by the Father. He told us they cultivated these flowers every year with great passion, as there was another purpose for their existence, the art of producing their own jam called 'Vartanoush' meaning 'sweet jam', made from the petals of the roses.

During spring thousands of jars of jam are prepared by the Fathers and because they come from this island, are connected to sanctity, they are sold out immediately.

It has also been told that several white peacocks roam around the grounds and we avidly looked for them but did not find them. They told us that they love to hide and then reappear only at their heart's desire, as they tended to be vain due to their regal splendid fantail. I then convinced myself that some other time I would be probably lucky enough to see this elegant bird, which represented 'immortality'.

Our tour continued with a visit to Lord Byron's chamber, a room which still remains unchanged, containing his desk, his pen, his manuscripts and a large plaque that reads: *'In memory of Lord Byron who was a Devoted Friend of the Armenians. He died for the liberation of Greece 1788-1824.*" He then joined the Greek War of Independence and fought against the Ottoman Turks.

Lord Byron traveled to Italy with his family and was in constant search of ways to rekindle his soul, learn self-discipline and flee from the tumultuous life. Upon learning about the 'serene' island, he paid a visit and loved it. One of his quotes says:

"The neatness, the comfort, the gentleness, the unaffected devotion, the accomplishments and the virtues of the brethren of the order, are well filled to strike the man of the world with the conviction that there are other and better things even in this life."

By visiting the island, he studied the culture of the Armenians, comprehended their hardship and decided to translate the Armenian grammar into English and develop an Armenian/English dictionary. His mind was busy daily with these accomplishments and it helped his mind and soul heal gradually, his outlook on life changed, his anger dissipated and humble approach towards life commenced. One of his quotes says it all: *"Always laugh when you can, it is cheap medicine."*

Now I leave you in the hands of My "Guardian Angels"

I think to myself, if I only had wings, then I would fly up high in the sky. I would soar to the heavens, glide through the stars and the planets, sprinkle angel dust and leave a trail of blissful sparkles on the earth, become a messenger of light and peace, and request the Lord to eternally protect and safeguard the children throughout the whole wide world.

My Artwork

Now the time has come for me to file the un-faded nostalgic memories, which I hope, have inspired you to perceive my nation in a different light and discover its many wonders.

PRESENTLY, I AM HAPPILY COMMITTED TO ACCOMPLISH MY MISSION ON EARTH AS IT IS MY DUTY TO REACH OUT AND SUPPORT CHILDREN IN NEED. PART OF THE PROCEEDS FROM THIS BOOK WILL GO TO:

'UNICEF'

UNITED NATIONS CHILDREN'S FUND

Thank you for reading this book

شكرا لكم على قرائة كتابي

This is not the end but the beginning of REDISCOVERING THE land between two rivers

A SPECIAL THANK YOU TO:

MANUEL CANERI, SEVAN CANERI,

LINDA OHANIAN, LINGUIST, ADVISER, TRANSLATOR, INTERPRETER WHO WAS
LIVING IN BAGHDAD DURING 2005-2011 AND REVISITED IN 2017.

PAPKEN KHATCHADOURIAN

SAIFELDIN AL ALOUSI

ZEIDOUN GABAR

I STOCK GETTY IMAGES

PIXABAY PHOTOS

UNSPLASH PHOTOS

DREAMSTIME PHOTOS

Printed in the United States
by Baker & Taylor Publisher Services